Personality and Science
An Interdisciplinary Discussion

A Ciba Foundation Report

Edited by
I. T. RAMSEY
and
RUTH PORTER

CHURCHILL LIVINGSTONE
Edinburgh and London
1971

First Published 1971

International Standard Book Number
0 7000 1523 X

Printed in Great Britain

17.1.72

Contents

v

Contributors

The Rt Revd I. T. Ramsey, Lord Bishop of Durham (*Chairman*)[1]
Auckland Castle, Bishop Auckland, Co. Durham, England

I. Chein
Department of Psychology, New York University, Washington Square, New York 3, N.Y. 10003, U.S.A.

S. Crown[1,2]
Department of Psychiatry, The London Hospital, Whitechapel, London E1 1BB, England

G. R. Dunstan[1]
Faculty of Theology, King's College London, Strand, London WC2R 2LS, England

M. A. Falconer
Neurosurgical Unit, The Maudsley Hospital, De Crespigny Park, Denmark Hill, London, S.E.5, England

P. Fourman[1,3]
University of Leeds Clinical Investigation Unit, The General Infirmary, Great George Street, Leeds 1, England

T. Freeman
Holywell Hospital, Antrim, N. Ireland

R. Greene
106 Harley Street, London W1N 1AF, England

R. M. Hare[1]
Corpus Christi College, Oxford, England

G. W. Harris
University of Oxford Department of Human Anatomy, South Parks Road, Oxford OX1 3QX, England

Sir Denis Hill[1,4]
Institute of Psychiatry, The Maudsley Hospital, De Crespigny Park, Denmark Hill, London, S.E.5, England

T. E. James[1,5]
Faculty of Laws, King's College London, Strand, London WC2R 2LS, England

C. R. B. Joyce[1]
Medical Department, CIBA-GEIGY Limited, 4002 Basle, Switzerland

S. Levine[6] Department of Psychiatry, Stanford University Medical Center, Stanford, California 94305, U.S.A.

B. G. Mitchell[1] Oriel College, Oxford, England

J. Owens All Saints' Hospital, Birmingham B18 5SD, England

R. S. Peters University of London Institute of Education, Malet Street, London WC1E 7HU, England

Ruth Porter (Rapporteur)[1] Ciba Foundation, London W1N 4BN, England

A. Ryle University Health Service, University of Sussex, Falmer, Brighton BN1 9QN, England

M. Schofield 28 Lyndhurst Gardens, Hampstead, London, N.W.3, England

G. K. Stürup Herstedvester Detention Centre for Abnormal Offenders, Albertslund, Denmark

T. Thompson Health Services Medical School, Department of Psychiatry, Minneapolis, Minnesota 55455, U.S.A.

R. F. Tredgold[1] Department of Psychological Medicine, University College Hospital, Gower Street, London WC1E 6AU, England

G. E. Vaillant Department of Psychiatry, Tufts-New England Medical Center, 171 Harrison Avenue, Boston, Massachusetts 02111, U.S.A.

O. H. Wolff[1,7] University of London Institute of Child Health, 30 Guilford Street, London WC1N 1EH, England

G. E. W. Wolstenholme[1] Ciba Foundation, London W1N 4BN, England

[1] Member of Working Party on Personality and Science which met thirteen times between May 1967 and October 1970.
[2] Co-opted November 1968.
[3] Died 8 October 1968.
[4] Resigned 6 November 1968.
[5] Co-opted October 1967.
[6] Presented material for the book after meetings of Working Party concluded.
[7] Co-opted December 1968.

The Ciba Foundation

The Ciba Foundation was opened in 1949 to promote international cooperation in medical and chemical research. It owes its existence to the generosity of CIBA Ltd, Basle (now CIBA-GEIGY Ltd), who, recognizing the obstacles to scientific communication created by war, man's natural secretiveness, disciplinary divisions, academic prejudices, distance, and differences of language, decided to set up a philanthropic institution whose aim would be to overcome such barriers. London was chosen as its site for reasons dictated by the special advantages of English charitable trust law (ensuring the independence of its actions), as well as those of language and geography.

The Foundation's house at 41 Portland Place, London, has become well known to workers in many fields of science. Every year the Foundation organizes six to ten three-day symposia and three to four shorter study groups, all of which are published in book form. Many other scientific meetings are held, organized either by the Foundation or by other groups in need of a meeting place. Accommodation is also provided for scientists visiting London, whether or not they are attending a meeting in the house.

The Foundation's many activities are controlled by a small group of distinguished trustees. Within the general framework of biological science, interpreted in its broadest sense, these activities are well summed up by the motto of the Ciba Foundation: *Consocient Gentes*—let the peoples come together.

1: Introduction

THE RT REVD DR I. T. RAMSEY,
LORD BISHOP OF DURHAM

FOR several years the Board for Social Responsibility of the Church of England took an initiative in setting up small interdisciplinary groups to discuss the morality of such issues as suicide, sterilization, the artificial prolongation of life and abortion. This initiative stemmed from a belief that moral decisions on these matters required the creative meeting of all the relevant disciplines which are needed for an adequate appraisal of such problems. These particular issues have been the subject of previous reports.[1-4] But it was agreed that there was need to explore a broader area where recent developments in medical science raise moral issues directly relating to the status and development of human personality. With the cooperation of the Ciba Foundation, London, meetings were therefore arranged at the Foundation between some of those who had participated in earlier groups and specialists in different scientific disciplines.*

At its first meeting the group decided that it might help most if the medical members could mention the developments in knowledge, or techniques, or practice which seemed most likely to invite philosophical and ethical comment, and this decision shaped the course of our discussion. Some developments concerned the use of medical knowledge in penal treatment. Although, in the case of some sexual offenders for example, there might be an argument for castration or sterilization based on considerations of social good, might not the enforcement of such treatment in prison compromise a man's personality? Alternatively, would it be morally more fitting for a man to be invited to have such treatment as a condition of release, the choice being then left to him? More generally, might not the imposition of treatment which was not for the patient's own good, but for the good of society, acutely raise the problem of where ought this principle to stop? These were but a few of the problems arising in the wider discussion of the use of medical procedures in penal treatment.

The issue of securing social good at the cost of possible personal impairment, or the infringing of individual rights, was also raised in connexion with the association of accident-proneness in driving and a high degree of masculinity or strong sexual impulses. Is it justifiable to reduce accidents by weakening those powers or modifying the behaviour

* For members of the working party and guest speakers see pp. vii–viii.

1

that makes a person distinctively a man? The same kind of conflict between the needs of society and the needs of the individual might arise with compulsory screening in order to detect and possibly to arrest antisocial pathological conditions. In this same context comes universal medication, for example fluoride added to drinking water or anti-malarial agents to salt. Of not least importance in this area is the whole question of medical participation in research in the context of bacteriological or chemical warfare. From the opposite direction, where the decision of the individual may bring undesirable social consequences, mention may be made of the growing social resort to tranquillizers, the medical and non-medical use of euphoric drugs, or the use of drugs to produce supernormality as in athletics, long-distance train driving or lorry driving.

Another area of discussion centred on the need to balance the chances of an unacceptable personality change against the chance of saving life or improving health. In this context, and taking the example of neuro-surgery, a distinction was drawn between: (*a*) the relief of a local diseased condition, for example a tumour; (*b*) relief from pain; and (*c*) the relief of mental illness as such, for example intense neurotic anxiety—the last being the most difficult problem of the three.

Another medical-moral issue of contemporary importance is clinical experimentation. The exploratory stage in the development of any medical procedure necessarily raises moral considerations beyond those of established medical practice. If there were no exploration, then presumably there would be no development and therefore no improve-ment in medical practice. But how can the exploration itself be morally controlled? The implanting of electrodes is but one example of an exploratory exercise and as with most explorations the patient, as well as the doctor, has decisions to make which involve his attitude to and evaluation of human existence.[5] On what grounds, for example, does a patient confronted by the possibility of a major transplant choose between a shorter life at one level of efficiency and a prolonged life at a lower level? What would a patient's choice be, and on what grounds would it be made, if he were to be told that aversion therapy for homo-sexuality might produce someone who was neither homosexual nor heterosexual?

One problem of interdisciplinary study and discussion is that those who are expert in various fields have to have the further qualification of communicating their views to others untrained in their respective disciplines, and to write in ways that these others can understand. The cost of interdisciplinary work is therefore that communications cannot display the full professional expertise of their writers. The writers of the papers in this book, whether these are scientific or not, are very much aware that if they had been written for their own professional circles the papers would be rather different. Whatever value belongs to these papers it is perhaps not improper to remind the reader of their particular purpose and character so that appropriate criteria for judgment can be used. Speaking more generally, it would betray a mistaken view of academic values if the papers of any interdisciplinary group were assumed to be necessarily substandard, as distinct from being of a different character altogether. The discussions and decisions of such groups have their own academic quality, and it is one which can be as high as their social and cultural importance. Just as technicalities do not guarantee detailed precision, neither does interdisciplinary work automatically depress academic standards. These reflections are not of course meant to stifle criticism of the present book, but rather to guard against unnecessary misunderstandings and point up a basic problem which interdisciplinary study always raises.

The present book offers to a wider public some of the thinking of our group as we have grappled with a few of these current medical problems and their wider implications. In the case of papers by specific authors, the authors themselves are of course alone responsible for the views expressed in them and they are not necessarily in agreement with opinions in discussions following their papers. Such account as is given of these discussions will, we hope, be helpful in high-lighting certain issues which we believe it would be worth-while to carry further. The discussion is reported verbatim on pp. 100–101 to reproduce a particular argument between two philosophers. None of the discussion represents any sort of final judgment on the topic under review. The book indeed represents the beginning not the end of a debate. There are many problems omitted, for example those associated with the bearing on personality of genetic engineering, euthanasia and contraception, and no problem is exhaustively treated. But we believe that the papers themselves and the topics we have raised in our preliminary discussion may help both to encourage a wider public to face important moral problems arising from contemporary developments in medicine and also to facilitate responsible debate on these topics.

As I have already implied, those who look for easy answers to particular topical problems in scientific medicine or for a clear-cut account of personality will be disappointed. (Indeed, much of the discussion is in the form of questions.) What we have rather tried to do (and what this book, as the outcome, offers to a wider public) has been to set out some of the recent developments in medical science and to give the initial reactions of the non-medical members of the group to these developments, as well as to recapitulate some of our discussions. We hope that the book will help readers, whether individually or as members of other interdisciplinary groups, to grapple all the better with some of these crucial problems in medicine and morality and to take forward the thinking and debate of this particular group, even though it is a journey on which, as we well realize, we have barely started.

We are most grateful for the generous hospitality, extending over more than three years, of the Ciba Foundation in making these discussions possible.

REFERENCES

1. CHURCH ASSEMBLY BOARD FOR SOCIAL RESPONSIBILITY (1959). *Ought Suicide to be a Crime?* London: Church Information Office.

2. CHURCH ASSEMBLY BOARD FOR SOCIAL RESPONSIBILITY (1962). *Sterilization: an Ethical Enquiry.* London: Church Information Office.

3. CHURCH ASSEMBLY BOARD FOR SOCIAL RESPONSIBILITY (1965). *Decisions about Life and Death: a Problem in Modern Medicine.* London: Church Information Office.

4. CHURCH ASSEMBLY BOARD FOR SOCIAL RESPONSIBILITY (1965). *Abortion: an Ethical Discussion.* London: Church Information Office.

5. LANDAU, R. L. (1967). *Perspect. Biol. Med.* **10**, 137. (Civil Rights and Clinical Investigator.)

2: On Becoming Male*

SEYMOUR LEVINE

IN the beginning there was female. All the available evidence leads to the conclusion that in development the process of becoming a male involves a number of complicated steps which are unnecessary in order for femaleness to occur. Thus the basic primordial sexual differentiation of most mammalian species is female, and a number of additive steps in the developmental process are essential to produce those changes in reproductive physiology and behaviour that characterize the male.

At least four major events are needed for the developing embryo to become male. If any of these is altered significantly the tendency of the embryo is to continue in its development as a female or a genetic male with many female characteristics. Initially, for maleness to occur at all, an X and a Y chromosome must be present in the genes, as compared to the development of the female in which there is a double X chromosome. In humans, 46 chromosomes are normally found. The major difference chromosomally between the male and the female is the presence of a Y chromosome in the male and its absence in the female. Human beings with only 45 chromosomes have only one X chromosome and no Y chromosome. Such XO persons are female. Other individuals have been found to have 47 chromosomes because they have two X chromosomes and a Y chromosome. Such XXY persons are male. The Y chromosome determines maleness—normally in XY individuals, abnormally in XXY individuals. The absence of the Y chromosome determines femaleness, normally in XX individuals, abnormally in XO individuals. This, then, is the first step in what we have called an additive process: the addition of a Y chromosome is necessary to initiate the very process of maleness.

The next critical event in becoming a male is the formation of the male gonads, the testes. The mammalian sex organs initially appear in the foetus as two ridges of tissue—the genital ridges. Each ridge has an inner mass of tissue, the medulla, and an outer mass of tissue, the cortex. This indifferent gonad can go in the direction either of formation of an ovary or of the more crucial male sex organ, the testis. If the medulla begins to reorganize itself the cortex atrophies and disappears and the resulting organ is a testis; conversely, if the cortex develops and the

* Paper contributed for publication (but not actually presented) after consultation with Professor Geoffrey Harris who had presented similar material informally to the working party.

medulla retrogresses the resulting gonad is an ovary. The formation of the testis in development precedes the formation of the ovary. There is little information as to the mechanism whereby the indifferent genital ridge becomes either testis or ovary but some active process does seem to be necessary for the medullary tissue to develop. If this process does not occur the organism's indifferent genital ridge tends to develop as an ovary.

Once the testes are formed, however, further vital steps are needed for the organism to become totally male. The foetal testes must secrete, first, a duct-organizing substance and, second, male hormones (androgens) in order for the embryo to become male. The secretion of a substance from the foetal male testis is essential for both anatomical and functional differentiation of the male. During intrauterine life the foetus is equipped with the *primordia* of both male and female genital ducts. The Müllerian ducts serve as an analogue of the uterus and Fallopian tubes, whereas the Wolffian ducts have the potentiality for differentiating further into the epididymis, vas deferens, seminal vesicles and ejaculatory duct of the male. In the human, during the third foetal month, either the Müllerian or Wolffian ducts complete their own development while involution occurs simultaneously in the opposite structures.[6] Secretions from the foetal testes play a decisive role in determining the direction of genital-duct development. In the presence of functional testes the Müllerian structures involute while the Wolffian ducts complete their development, whereas in the absence of the testes the Wolffian ducts are reabsorbed and the Müllerian structures mature.

Female development is not contingent on the presence of an ovary, since equally good development of the uterus and Fallopian tubes will take place if no ovary is present. The influence of the foetal testes on duct development is unilateral since early removal of one testis leads to Müllerian development on that side while the male duct develops normally on the side on which the testis is intact. The systemic injection of androgen to a young embryo fails to duplicate the action of the foetal testes. When extremely high doses of androgen are applied locally the Wolffian ducts exhibit signs of stimulation, but no inhibitory effect on Müllerian elements has been observed. These data have led to the belief that the foetal testes secrete a duct-organizing substance which is distinct from ordinary androgen.

The presence of normal male anatomical structure still does not ensure that the developing embryo will become functionally male. What do we mean by the concept 'functionally male'? If we examine in detail some of the major differences between male and female sexuality we note that there are sex dimorphisms in many aspects of reproductive physiology, stress physiology, metabolic processes and behaviour. In particular, with regard to reproductive physiology and the behavioural aspects of maleness and femaleness, one of the principal actions of

6

androgen during development seems to be the organization of the immature central nervous system (CNS) into the male type. Once again we are talking about an active process: the presence of androgen during development acts upon the brain to programme, in effect, patterns of maleness. The absence of androgen permits the ongoing process of femaleness to pursue its natural course. The evidence to support this theory is now abundant.

One of the principal distinctions between males and females with regard to reproductive physiology is the cyclic pattern of ovulation in the female of most mammalian species and its absence in the male. The human female ovulates about once every 28 days, the guinea-pig about once every 15 and the rat once every 4 to 5 days. This process is regulated by hormones from the anterior pituitary gland. In cyclic fashion the anterior pituitary delivers to the ovary a follicle-stimulating hormone (FSH); this promotes the growth of the Graafian follicle which produces oestrogen and also houses the ova, to be released at the times of ovulation. The anterior pituitary also releases luteinizing hormone (LH) which induces the formation of the corpora lutea and triggers ovulation. The formation of corpora lutea is clear evidence that ovulation has occurred. There is a continuing ongoing feedback system which is only interrupted in the normal 'cycling' female by the onset of pregnancy. The male, in contrast, shows no such cyclicity. His testes continually receive LH from the anterior pituitary but in the male LH causes the development of the interstitial cells of the testes, those cells which are predominantly responsible for testosterone production. The pattern of hormone production from the anterior pituitary of the female is cyclic in order to maintain the process of ovulation. The process of production of hormones in the male is for the most part non-cyclic.

The pituitary gland is in itself not sexually differentiated. If a female pituitary is transplanted into a male, normal male functions will be maintained and, conversely, if the male pituitary is transplanted into a normal female, complete female function will also be maintained. The implications of these findings are that pituitary regulation does not come from the pituitary itself but from some other controlling mechanism. All the available evidence indicates that these controlling mechanisms are somewhere in the CNS. The clearest demonstration of the role of the testes in modulating CNS control of reproduction comes from studies in which newborn rats have been deprived of their testes. It has been dramatically demonstrated, most recently by Professor Geoffrey Harris,[3, 4] that when these neonatally castrated males are allowed to grow, their pattern of anterior pituitary release of those hormones which regulate gonadal function (FSH and LH) is cyclic and indistinguishable from that of a normal female. If an ovary is transplanted into an adult male animal which has been castrated as a newborn, this ovary shows full cyclic ovulation. Thus, in such a case, a genetic male with XY chromosomes, a morphological male showing full sexual differentiation of anatomical structures, is still responding, in terms of the CNS, as a female. It should be noted that if, following castration, the male is given a single injection of testosterone, the ovulation that is seen in adulthood no longer occurs. Furthermore, if the newborn female is given a single injection of testosterone shortly after birth she is also non-cyclic and incapable of maintaining the normal patterns of ovulation. These studies provide one line of evidence which indicates that maleness is dependent on the presence of a male CNS and that, in order to have a male CNS, the foetal and neonatal testes must secrete androgen, which presumably acts upon the brain to differentiate it into the male type. There are definite critical periods in development for these events to occur. If the newborn male rat is castrated within 24 hours of birth the CNS will continue to be female. But if this period exceeds approximately 72 hours the male CNS has been permanently and irreversibly established.

The hypothesis of sexual differentiation of the brain is further substantiated when one examines the influence on adult sexual behaviour of the presence or absence of testosterone in both the newborn male and female rat. In most mammalian species the hormones emanating from the ovary and the testis exert profound control on sexual behaviour. In normal circumstances the female rat becomes sexually receptive during a period in the oestrous cycle when there exists the appropriate hormonal balance between the ovarian hormones, oestrogen and progesterone, that results in ovulation. If the female is deprived of the appropriate circulating hormones by ovariectomy, sexual receptivity is immediately abolished. However, when the appropriate hormones are replaced, either by sustained high doses of oestrogen or by small doses of oestrogen followed by progesterone, sexual behaviour appears within a very short time after the progesterone administration.

Sexual behaviour of the male rat involves a much more complex pattern of mounts with intromissions and ejaculation. In contrast to the cyclic pattern of receptivity shown by the female, the male rat is acyclic in its sexual behaviour and will in normal circumstances copulate as long as there is an appropriate stimulus object. The biological adaptiveness of these two different patterns is readily apparent. For the female of most mammalian species sexual receptivity is consistent with ovulation so that almost every sexual contact would result in pregnancy. But if the male also had a cyclic pattern of sexual activity, the conditions under which pregnancy would occur would, in the least, be infinitely more complex. Again, in contrast to the female, when the male rat is castrated there ensues a period of time during which it is sexually active even in the absence of circulating hormones. Eventually the animal will cease normal sexual activity, but following replacement with testosterone will resume behaviour that is indistinguishable from that of the normal intact male. However, no amount of oestrogen and progesterone has yet proved capable of reliably eliciting in the adult castrate male patterns of sexual behaviour typical of the normal female.

The evidence regarding normal patterns of sexual behaviour and their dependency upon circulating hormones is consistent with the hypothesis that there are differences between the male and female brain with regard to patterns of hormone secretion and behaviour. Thus, female sexual receptivity in the rat is easily elicited with the appropriate regime of oestrogen and progesterone replacements following removal of the ovary. In the male these behaviours appear to be completely suppressed and cannot be elicited with doses of oestrogen and progesterone that are a thousandfold higher than those required in the female.[7] These findings show that one of the primary aspects of sexual differentiation in the rat appears to be suppression of the capacity in the normal male to respond to oestrogen and progesterone.

Although there is a firm underlying assumption that behaviour reflects in some ways the action of the CNS, there is clear evidence that sex hormones can act directly on the brain. Implants of synthetic oestrogen (stilboestrol) in one area of the brain—the hypothalamus—of the female cat evoke female sexual behaviour, although the cat does not show the usual physiological signs of oestrus. In similar experiments implants of testosterone in the brains of castrated male rats also elicited male sexual behaviour, although again there was no sign of the effect of this testosterone on the anatomical structures of the male reproductive system. The influence on sexual behaviour patterns of androgen administered during development is demonstrated by the two now classic approaches to the problem: the administration of testosterone to an organism which normally would not have testosterone—that is, the female—or the removal of the testosterone-producing organs, the testes, during a critical period in the development of the male. In the case of the female, a single injection of testosterone can abolish female patterns of sexual receptivity. A female thus injected not only fails to show any signs of sexual receptivity in normal circumstances but also, when the ovary is removed, sexual behaviour cannot be elicited by the appropriate replacement with oestrogen and progesterone. This hormonal replacement would normally elicit complete sexual receptivity in non-testosterone-treated ovariectomized females. Further, if these females are treated neonatally with testosterone they will show some increase in male patterns of sexual behaviour following injections of androgen in adulthood.[5] Conversely, although it is extremely difficult if not impossible to elicit female receptivity in a male that has been castrated as an adult, if the testes are removed within 24 hours of birth

9

sexual responses elicited by oestrogen and progesterone administered in adulthood are completely indistinguishable from these responses in a normal female. Not only are they indistinguishable to the human observer but normal adult males will respond to these oestrogen- and progesterone-treated neonatally castrated males as if they were females in heat. Once again, a single injection of testosterone given shortly after castration to the newborn animal will completely reverse all these effects.

We have thus far assumed that the function of gonadal hormones in infancy is to organize the CNS with regard to neuroendocrine control of behaviour. Although we have focused primarily on reproductive behaviour numerous reports in the literature have indicated that there are sex differences in non-sexual behaviour. Indeed, if we are to make a convincing argument that the effects of androgen are to influence the CNS, then it seems reasonable to assume that other patterns of sex differences would also be influenced by these same hormones. There are now well-reported differences[3] in activity patterns between males and females. Activity patterns of the female closely parallel oestrous cycle activity and during the oestrous phase of the cycle females show high peaks of activity. In contrast, the male shows no apparent activity cycle and overall activity levels are much lower. These female activity cycles can be mimicked in the neonatally castrated male by an ovarian transplant in adulthood. Thus, before the transplantation of the ovary, the male which has been castrated as a newborn shows a low level of random activity. However, the appearance of corpora lutea in the transplanted ovary marks the onset of female activity cycles which are again indistinguishable from those of normal females. During this period the neonatally castrated rat with the transplanted ovary also becomes sexually receptive on a cyclic basis. Sex dimorphisms have also been noted in other patterns of behaviour, including emotional responses to novel situations and aggressive behaviour.

Recently we have investigated the effects of androgen on experimentally induced aggressive behaviour.[1] Male and female rats differ markedly in the amount of aggressive behaviour elicited by exposure to electric shock, with males fighting significantly more than females. Further, if males are castrated at weaning their aggressive behaviour is reduced but not quite to the level seen in normal females. When they receive replacement treatment with testosterone these males show significant increases in aggressive behaviour equivalent to that observed in the normal intact male. The female, however, shows no increase in aggressive behaviour following testosterone treatment. In male rats castrated as newborns, aggressive behaviour is suppressed and supramaximal doses of androgen given to the adult animal do not increase aggressive behaviour as is seen in castrated weanling rats. Here is another example of the maintenance of feminine patterns of behaviour when the newborn male is castrated. Further, there appears in this experiment that property of the CNS which has been observed throughout many of the experiments discussed thus far, namely, that the female brain is differentially responsive to androgen and that many behaviours which are elicited by androgen in normal males are generally incapable of appearing on androgen stimulation of the normal female or of its equivalent, the male that has been castrated during the critical period in development.

Examination of developmental patterns of the testis indicates that during the late prenatal periods, and in the rat for a brief period of time postnatally, the foetal and neonatal testis exhibits a high degree of endocrine activity, with active production of testosterone. But after this brief period of activity the testis becomes quiescent and little androgen is produced until just before puberty. One can infer that this period of high androgen activity during a critical period in development is essential for the sexual differentiation of the brain.

For obvious reasons the research we have discussed thus far has been accomplished mainly in laboratory animals. In man the closest analogue to demonstrate the influence of testosterone during development on subsequent sexuality is the syndrome of testicular feminization.[8] In this syndrome the internal ducts are predominantly male but the external genitalia resemble those of the female, although the vagina is shallow and ends blindly in a pouch. At adolescence, female secondary sex characteristics develop—notably, well-developed breasts and rounding of the body contours. The aetiology of this disorder can be attributed to a peculiar process by which the target tissues become androgen resistant. Thus, although the testes produce the appropriate hormones the tissues apparently remain insensitive to androgen and consequently the syndrome of overt feminization is produced.

The clinical literature abounds with numerous instances of gender role reversals caused by pathological conditions, with resultant sexual ambiguities, in particular penile-like structures in female offspring. But it has been clearly demonstrated by Professor John Money and his group[2] that, to a very large extent, the gender role assigned to the individual born with distorted external genitalia is dependent on the way in which he or she is reared. Thus, if the individual with such sexual ambiguity is treated as a male, it will generally assume a male gender role, although it may indeed have ovaries. Conversely, if the individual is brought up as a female, it will thus continue female, although again the internal genitalia and chromosomal patterns may be those of a male. Thus, at least as far as the human being is concerned, an additional process occurs in development which involves the establishment of gender role as a function of learning.

11

What I have tried to demonstrate in this paper is that in order for maleness to occur there are several unique active processes which must take place with exquisite timing during development. As Professor A. Jost (personal communication) recently stated: "it is a struggle to become a male." This initial struggle is apparently only the beginning.

REFERENCES

1. CONNER, R. L. and LEVINE, S. (1969). In *Aggressive Behaviour*, p. 150, eds Garattini, S. and Sigg, E. B. Amsterdam: Excerpta Medica.
2. HAMPSON, J. L. (1965). In *Sex and Behaviour*, p. 108, ed. Beach, F. A. New York: Wiley.
3. HARRIS, G. W. (1964). *Endocrinology* 75, 627.
4. HARRIS, G. W. and LEVINE, S. (1962). *J. Physiol., Lond.* 163, 42P.
5. HARRIS, G. W. and LEVINE, S. (1965). *J. Physiol., Lond.* 163, 42.
6. HARRIS, G. W., MICHAEL, R. P. and SCOTT, P. P. (1958). In *Ciba Fdn Symp. Neurological Basis of Behaviour*, p. 236, eds Wolstenholme, G.E. W. and O'Connor, C. M. London: Churchill.
7. JOST, A. (1958). In *Hermaphroditism, Genital Anomalies and Related Endocrine Disorders*, p. 15, eds Jones, H. W. and Scott, W. W. Baltimore: Williams and Wilkins.
8. SIMMER, H. H., PION, R. J. and DIGNAM, W. J. (1965). *Testicular Feminization*. Chicago, Ill.: Thomas.

3: Disturbances of Behaviour in Endocrine Disorder

RAYMOND GREENE

THIS paper has a text. A translation of something that Sigmund Freud wrote in about 1938[1] reads thus: "The future may teach us how to exercise a direct influence, by means of particular chemical substances, upon the amounts of energy and their distribution in the apparatus of the mind. It may be that there are other undreamt-of possibilities of therapy. But for the moment we have nothing better at our disposal than the technique of psycho-analysis, and for that reason, in spite of its limitations, it is not to be despised."

Freud's disciples would do well to ponder the words of the Master. They have become, especially in the US, *plus papistes que le Pape*.

Freud's comment can of course be applied to the numerous psychotropic drugs now available. 'The amounts of energy' are changed by such exogenous drugs as the derivatives of barbituric acid on the one hand and of amphetamine on the other. Their 'distribution in the mental apparatus' is altered by, for instance, the tranquillizers and anti-depressants. But here I shall discuss 'chemical substances' that are endogenous—produced, that is, within the body itself by the ductless glands. Behaviour may be influenced by either overproduction or underproduction.

Here I must apologize to medical readers. Knowledge of this subject is often anecdotal, a word which in scientific ears has become pejorative. Yet most modern medical knowledge began in this way. In human economics, food gatherers preceded food producers, and so it has been with medicine. Hippocrates, in the fourth century B.C., did little but describe in admirable detail the things he saw. Much of the theory later called Hippocratic was probably added by his followers in later years. The theory of humours, for instance, in which all disease was discussed in terms of the four humours—phlegm, blood, yellow bile and black bile—was probably not Hippocratic at all.

The relationship between hormones and the nervous system is so close that the physiologist John Fulton once remarked to me that endocrinology is only a branch of neurology. The hypothalamus, an integral part of the nervous system, produces hormones that control the production of anterior pituitary hormones—the so-called releasing factors. The hypothalamus also produces the hormones believed in the past to arise in the posterior pituitary, where in fact they are merely stored.

13

The hypothalamus has ousted the anterior pituitary from its pride of place amongst the endocrine glands. Another link is provided by the catecholamines, which are produced not only by the adrenal medulla but also at the nerve endings of the autonomic nervous system. Moreover, the target endocrine glands, though mainly under the control of the trophic hormones of the anterior pituitary, are themselves subject to some degree of autonomic control.

In various human disorders the link between the systems is so close that it is often pointless to ask whether a disease is neurological or endocrinological. Emotional stress may precipitate thyrotoxicosis, exacerbate diabetes mellitus, stop or accentuate menstruation, or cause water retention in the tissues. These somatic results of mental strain all appear to be the end results of a chain of reactions that begins in the cortex of the brain and passes through the hypothalamus, pituitary gland and target glands to the periphery. An interesting question is why some individuals are more subject than others to this chain of reactions. If this question can be answered we shall be well on the way to an understanding of the psychosomatic disorders. No single mental illness is constantly associated with a single endocrine disorder. Perhaps some people spend their lives walking along a psychopathological tight rope from which they may be pushed either way by excess or deficiency of glandular function, to hit the ground with equal force whichever way they fall. Some individuals may be more ready than others to bring into operation their counter-stress mechanisms. Some may bring them into action with undue and damaging enthusiasm, while others are so calmly made that they only need to use these mechanisms in the most extreme circumstances.

SEX HORMONES

Although much of the relationship between the endocrine glands and the mind is of recent discovery, the effect of castration on human aggressiveness was well recognized in ancient times. The first experimental verification was by Berthold of Göttingen, who changed the cock into a submissive bird by castration and restored its aggressiveness by re-implanting its testes. Sir Gordon Holmes, an English neurologist in the nineteen-twenties, first recognized that masculine aggressiveness may supplant feminine submissiveness in the presence of an adrenal tumour producing an excess of male hormone. This change is commonly seen when the proportion of female to male hormones is naturally diminished in women at the menopause, and its converse is observed often in the 'mellowing' of the ageing man. These changes in character may be related to the effects of the sex hormones on the hypothalamus. The amygdaloid nucleus, one of the basal nuclei of the cerebrum, contains an aggression centre, electrical stimulation of which can turn aggressive behaviour on and off. The amygdaloid nucleus can be affected by sights, sounds and smells, and by hormones. A raging bull can be converted into a gentle steer by castration. When two male mice meet they usually begin to fight, invariably if they have been isolated. Females and castrated males are less aggressive. If castrated males are treated with testosterone they become hostile but females do not unless they have been given testosterone from birth.

Although recent history has thrown doubt on the idea that essential differences exist between the behavioural reactions of man and of the so-called lower animals, it remains true that it is unwise to transfer from one animal to another the lessons learned. Anthropomorphism has bedevilled our observations about the behaviour of species other than our own, and the reverse statement also applies. The old lady who attributes human instincts and thought processes to her Pekinese dog is committing in reverse the mistake of the experimental worker who extrapolates from the non-human primate, or even from insect, bird and various mammals, to man. Nevertheless, many common features in the behaviour of vertebrates are mediated by hormonal action and this may occasionally be true of man.

Thus it has been shown that dogs and cats deprived of their cerebral hemispheres are still capable of copulation and fertility. Study of the human race suggests that this is also true of men and women. It may even be said that these functions are increased in those whose cerebral capacity is low. The lordosis of the female, the palpation and pelvic thrust, the hopping and wiggling of the ears, all so typical of the female rat in a state of sexual receptivity, may be observed on any evening on any dance floor. The back-kicking of the unreceptive female rat is in such circumstances rarely observed. In the male rat cerebral damage of such a degree that sexual interest dies may be repaired by the injection of testosterone. It is unfortunate that this hormone fails to produce a similar effect in man. In the female rat and cat, on the other hand, removal of the whole cerebral cortex fails to reduce the copulatory response. But in the human species the temporary ablation of the cortex by alcohol, though it may fail to reduce the female response, may seriously impair that of the male, as the porter in *Macbeth* so correctly observed four centuries ago. In the male, compared with the female, the higher centres seem to play a larger part than the endocrine glands in sexual behaviour. Male apes castrated in infancy display a speed and frequency of copulation that compares favourably with the performance of the intact animal, and in the human species the eunuch is not necessarily impotent. On the other hand, removal of the ovaries from the female rat completely eliminates her sexual responses whereas the virtual death of the ovaries in the human female in middle age does not necessarily do so.

15

Ninon de l'Enclos at the age of 80, when asked by her grand-daughter, "When does a woman cease to feel the pangs of love?" is said to have answered, "I do not yet know." Even in women the cortex seems to play its part.

The problems of puberty and adolescence have recently been brought to the fore by the violent and apparently insensate behaviour of students in recent demonstrations. It seems likely that the *apparent* causes of their misdemeanours are unimportant. The war in Vietnam, the demand for student power in the government of universities, opposition to nuclear warfare and the pros and cons of racial segregation are probably only pegs on which the adolescent hangs his desire to be of the crowd and to avoid the growing necessity to be an individual—lonely and responsible. Moreover, the increased feeling of aggression caused by a flood of testosterone to which his brain has not yet learned to adapt itself must find an outlet. Intellectual development tends to lag behind sexual development, and social development behind intellectual development. That these stages in maturation are partly of endocrine origin is suggested by animal experiments in which it has been found that castration reduces the capacity of the male rat to learn, a reduction that can be corrected by testosterone. In the spayed female rat oestradiol reduces the capacity to learn, an effect that can be neutralized by testosterone. It is doubtful if these observations are relevant to human beings, but one observation suggests that they do have some validity. The clinical endocrinologist frequently sees the boy who is sexually, somatically and scholastically backward. His genitalia are unduly small, his height is below the normal for his age and his form-mates are younger than he is. Treatment aimed at increasing his sexual development has as a by-product an acceleration of growth due to the anabolic activity of androgens. The boy's scholastic achievement almost invariably increases as well, often to the pleased surprise of his masters. It sometimes seems that before puberty a boy only works if he is forced to do so. Later the mind matures and he begins to see that work is not only necessary but may be interesting. This change may be due to other causes but the increased aggressiveness produced by testosterone may help to bring about this improvement. The unhappiness felt by the boy who is too small to stand up to his fellows may have been a handicap in the past. The psychological effects of being different are often underrated by doctors who assure the parents that eventually all will be well. 'Leave it to nature' is the advice most commonly given. The misery suffered is neglected: its effects may last for life.

At the other end of the span of reproductive life, the climacteric may have profound emotional effects. Whether there exists in the male a phase of rapidly diminishing testicular function is doubtful. Excretory studies suggest that a very gradual diminution in the secretion of testosterone occurs in middle and old age, and it is doubtful whether this is related to the psychological changes that undoubtedly occur in some elderly men. Occasionally they experience a wide variety of symptoms, such as emotional instability, irritability, sudden changes in mood, failing memory and concentration, decreased interest in their usual activities and severe depression. It must be remembered that there are often sound psychological causes for these symptoms. The man in whose past life sex has been a major interest finds his attraction for women beginning to wane and his capacity for sexual response growing smaller. He may have concentrated unduly on his work and may now find it difficult to fill his days. If games once occupied his mind unduly he may be depressed by his lessening skill. As he approaches his three score years and ten he finds his friends growing fewer because they die. He himself may begin to fear death for his own sake or for others.

In women it is otherwise. The fall in ovarian activity is relatively sudden. The same causes of psychological symptoms may operate as in the male but to these are added physical symptoms that may be very disturbing, such as hot flushes, attacks of excessive sweating, excessive and irregular menstrual bleeding and painful changes in the skin of the genital area. The combination of the two factors, psychological and physical, may make life unbearable for the patient and her family. Fortunately severe symptoms are comparatively rare. The majority of women pass through the climacteric unscathed and the symptoms are easily controlled by hormones if necessary.

It is important to realize that 16 per cent of women simply stop menstruating (for many of them this is a welcome relief) and experience no menopausal symptoms. Only 10 per cent are sufficiently incapacitated to need treatment. The symptoms reported are flushes (62 per cent), headache (45 per cent), occasional vertigo (40 per cent), increasing weight (34 per cent), moodiness (31 per cent), rheumatic pains (24 per cent) and floodings (21 per cent). These symptoms occur most often at 50 years of age, but in 8 per cent of women they start before 40 years and in 5 per cent after 55 years. There is no known reason why a few women should have these symptoms severely and a few not at all. Marriage or celibacy, child birth or infertility, previous good health or bad, affect the issue not at all. One thing does, however, affect it. In Montaigne's words: "Who feareth to suffer, suffereth already because he feareth." The late Joan Malleson quoted one old woman who said, "I have had a lot of trouble in my time and most of it never happened."

Homosexuality has been suspected of having an endocrine origin but there was no scientific evidence for this until 1970, when Loraine and co-workers[2] reported abnormally low testosterone levels in the urine of two out of three male homosexuals, and raised urinary luteinizing hormone and testosterone and low urinary oestrogens in three out of four female homosexuals. The authors made no particular claims for the significance of these observations but they are undoubtedly interesting and worth further study. The male homosexual, however, does not become heterosexual when treated with testosterone nor does the Lesbian when treated with ovarian hormones. Testosterone treatment may increase the sex drive in either sex, but its direction is not reversed. Homosexuals reach puberty at the usual age and physical examination of the adult shows no sign of endocrine abnormality. Homosexuality is not unduly common in individuals known to have an abnormal ratio of sex hormones.

ADRENAL CORTICAL HORMONES

Much of the recent work stems from the research of Hans Selye whose concept envisages a wide variety of stresses (not only physical shocks but also more sustained mental strains) each producing an effect upon the body as a whole through the hormones, especially those of the adrenal cortex. The strain of public speaking, of waiting for a surgical operation, of military combat or of the varsity boat race all increase urinary and blood levels of adrenal cortical hormones.

Cushing's syndrome, due to excessive activity of the adrenal cortex, is often accompanied by psychological changes, even complete insanity. I have seen a very able woman become insane before the diagnosis of Cushing's syndrome was made. When I first saw her, her mind was completely divorced from reality. Her adrenal glands were removed and by the time she recovered from the anaesthetic she was mentally normal. The psychological effects of Addison's disease, in which the adrenal cortex is deficient, may also be profound. Apathy, negativism, seclusiveness, depression and irritability occur in about half the cases. Undue suspiciousness and agitation are fairly common and delusions occasionally occur. Manic-depressive psychosis may be in some way related to the adrenal cortex, for the blood of patients in a manic state has been found to prolong the life of animals whose adrenal glands have been removed. There may be some relationship between the adrenal cortex and those periodical attacks of insanity in which gross water retention occurs, deterioration in mental state seeming to coincide with the days on which the weight is highest.

BLOOD SUGAR

The mental effects of a low blood sugar provide a good example of the variety of results due to changes in a single substance. Some mental or nervous effects are invariably seen when the blood sugar is lowered by an insulin-secreting tumour of the pancreas, in Addison's disease or in so-called idiopathic hypoglycaemia. At one end of the scale are fatigue, anxiety, restlessness, irritability and a feeling of tension; in the middle lie automatic activity, confusion, loss of memory, 'drunken' behaviour and negativism; and at the other end mania, violence, hallucinations, delirium, delusions and coma may be seen. The mental effects of a low blood sugar seem to depend not only on the actual level but on the way the brain reacts to it. Brain function depends on the availability of glucose. Chronic hypoglycaemia is not always readily diagnosed. In one famous case a young man of unstable character, whose blood sugar was low because of a prolonged fast, stabbed his mother to death. A woman received prolonged psychiatric treatment for a tendency to become noisy, abusive and violent with no provocation, until a discerning psychiatrist became suspicious and referred her to an endocrine clinic where she was cured by the removal of a pancreatic tumour.

PARATHYROID HORMONE

The pancreas is not the only organ the disordered function of which can induce dementia. Not only a low blood sugar but a low blood calcium may on occasions have a strangely similar effect. The fact that it does so rather uncommonly suggests that this abnormality of blood chemistry, due to an idiopathic reduction in the activity of the parathyroid glands or to their surgical removal (purposeful or accidental), is activating a previous mental abnormality rather than creating a new one. The originally sound mind retains its balance, the unsteady one falls off its tight rope. Depression, loss of interest in surrounding things and people, lack of personal care, vertigo, anxiety and epilepsy may occur. One woman who suffered from a tumour of a parathyroid gland had the brittle bones usual in this disease. The tumour was removed and the blood calcium fell from an unduly high to an unduly low level. Although this was quickly rectified she became confused and began to suffer from strange delusions. She thought she was in hell and that the other patients in the ward were devils sent to plague her. A psychiatrist was called in with a view to transferring her to a mental hospital. She formed the highly erroneous opinion that he was Christ, come to rescue her and escort her to heaven. He reported that she was hopelessly and permanently insane and left the ward to make the necessary arrangements for her transfer. As he left the ward she rushed to follow him, slipped, fell heavily, and broke her still brittle femur. Within a minute she was perfectly sane, providing an interesting example of shock therapy applied by the patient herself.

High parathyroid function, due usually to a tumour, also affects the mind in about 50 per cent of patients. The mental disturbances consist of lack of initiative, and of depression and acute organic psychosis in

19

the most severe cases. The mental disturbances are wholly reversible when the blood calcium returns to normal after successful extirpation of the parathyroid adenoma. Mental changes and serum calcium levels are correlated: the higher the serum calcium the more severe is the mental disturbance.

BLOOD POTASSIUM

Depression is common when the blood potassium level, also under endocrine control, falls too low. This is seen in Cushing's disease, when it is due to overactivity of the adrenal cortex, but it also occurs when too little potassium is present in the diet, when vomiting is profuse, and when diuretics and purgatives are abused.

Perhaps in this wildly speculative field of study the relationship between depression and potassium deficiency is the nearest we can get to relating definitely a chemical (often endocrine) abnormality with a mental state.

ADRENAL MEDULLARY HORMONES

Recently there has been some hope that the chemistry of anxiety may be similarly pinned down. It has recently been shown that after exercise (which raises the level of lactate in the blood) anxious patients experienced an undue rise of lactate and, concomitantly, feelings of dread and causeless fear of, for example, a heart attack or death. If lactate is infused into normal subjects until the serum level is ten times the normal value, they experience typical attacks of anxiety that can be prevented by the simultaneous infusion of calcium. The authors suggested that anxiety states occur in normal people if the serum lactate rises too high in response to an increased release of adrenaline. Many of the symptoms of anxiety can certainly be produced by the injection of adrenaline which may evoke a profound emotional disturbance even in normal people but especially so in subjects with an anxiety neurosis. Conversely, some well-balanced people may experience a pleasant thrill when slight fear in controllable circumstances raises their output of adrenaline. Perhaps this explains the fascination of rock-climbing, and racing on horses or in motor cars.

Schizophrenia may be related to endocrine dysfunction. Thudichum wrote in the nineteenth century: "Many forms of insanity are unquestionably the external manifestations of the effects upon the brain substance of poisons fermented within the body. . . . These poisons we shall, I have no doubt, be able to isolate after we know the normal chemistry to its utmost detail. And then will come in their turn the crowning discoveries to which our efforts must ultimately be directed, namely, the discoveries of the antidotes to the poisons and to the fermenting causes and processes which produce them." The effects of mescaline mimic the natural disorder in some ways and, since mescaline is chemically similar to adrenaline, it has been suggested that schizophrenics might have an abnormality of adrenaline metabolism that results in the production of an abnormal metabolite with an action similar to that of mescaline.

THYROID HORMONES

Hyperthyroidism tends to make a patient more irritable, anxious and excitable than he previously was because thyroxine increases the excitability of the sympathetic nervous system. Conversely, hypothyroidism slows down the sympathetic nervous system and tends to make the patient slower in his emotional reactions than he was in the past. However, the effects of too much or too little circulating thyroxine must be looked upon merely as effects upon the previous personality. The mood of the previously highly excitable person may be raised to an almost manic level should he develop thyrotoxicosis, whereas the mood of the previously phlegmatic person may be raised only to normal. And the mood of the previously excitable person may be reduced to a normal level by hypothyroidism, the previously phlegmatic person becoming still more calm.

Myxoedema, caused by a profound decrease in thyroid activity, sometimes has other effects: it may give rise to extreme irritability, perhaps due to the frustration of an active mind that realizes its new incompetence. Worse things may occur. Though fully developed myxoedema may be easy to diagnose just from the appearance of the patient, this is not always so easy. Many cases of psychosis severe enough for incarceration in mental hospitals are undoubtedly due to thyroid deficiency. Such patients may remain undiagnosed and rot for years in such institutions before a perspicacious psychiatrist makes the correct diagnosis. The madness may take many forms. In 1888 a committee of the Clinical Society of London recorded that "delusions and hallucinations occur in nearly half the cases, mainly where the disease is advanced. Insanity as a complication is noted in about the same proportion as delusions and hallucinations. It takes the form of acute or chronic manias, dementia, or melancholia, with a marked predominance of suspicion and self-accusation." Paranoia and severe confusion may also occur resulting in extremely violent behaviour. Should the condition be undiagnosed the damage may be permanent, but even after many years as a certified lunatic a patient may be cured by thyroxine, and return to a useful life. In lesser degrees of psychological abnormality the presence of thyroid deficiency may be easily overlooked.

21

Students are too often trained to think only of the most severe symptoms and to expect to see them all together in every patient. In fact there is no symptom or sign of thyroid deficiency that may not be absent and in many instances only one of these may be present. That single symptom or sign may be a disorder of behaviour or of thought.

The cretin shows the effect on the brain of prolonged thyroid deficiency from birth. Thyroxine is necessary for the development of the brain. If treatment is begun within a few weeks of birth the cretin may progress sufficiently to grow into an adult not obviously different from his fellows, but the effects of thyroid deficiency before birth are rarely completely reversed and he never becomes outstandingly intelligent. If the diagnosis is not made for months or years, the hope of completely normal mental development progressively recedes. The mental deficiency of the adult cretin is often strangely patchy. Sudden flashes of intelligence may momentarily illuminate the darkness of his mind. But he is usually childlike and his emotions are labile and uninhibited. He is often thoughtlessly cruel and spiteful, or pathetically dependent.

ANOREXIA NERVOSA

This is a condition in which neurology, psychiatry and endocrinology are closely intermingled. The patient, usually a young girl, decides to starve for reasons unknown or known only to herself. Often the obvious (but not necessarily true) beginning of the illness is an obsessional wish to be more slim, occasionally because mother is fat and the common mother-daughter antagonism of the teens dictates a desire to be as unlike mother as possible. The main clinical features are profound loss of appetite resulting in emaciation. In women (the patient is usually female) amenorrhoea is always present. Menstruation is singularly sensitive to psychic factors. Probationer nurses, fresh from home and precipitated suddenly into new surroundings, may cease to menstruate for many months. It is not uncommon for a young girl who has for the first time risked pregnancy to miss her next period and go in unnecessary panic to her doctor or hide herself away in miserable contemplation of a pregnancy that does not exist. Usually the causes of anorexia nervosa are undetectable; but the results are serious. The pituitary reduces its output of trophic hormones and the other endocrine glands fail progressively. Does starvation come first and cause a protective reflex in the hypothalamus which in its turn reduces the activity of the ductless glands? Since psychological treatment and, if necessary, forced feeding cure many such patients it would seem that this is a reasonable explanation. Or does a hypothalamic lesion produce anorexia and endocrine deficiency simultaneously? The fact that undoubted evidence of endocrine deficiency may be seen before loss of weight supports this view. Perhaps both explanations are true, one for one type of patient and the other for another.

I have probably asked more questions than I have answered in this discursive review of some of the changes in behaviour that may be associated with endocrine disorders. A great deal more research is needed in these areas.

REFERENCES

1. FREUD, S. (1938). *Abriss der Psychoanalyse* (1963). In *An Outline of Psychoanalysis*, p. 48, trans. Strachey, J. London: Hogarth Press.
2. LORAINE, J. A., ISMAIL, A. A. A., ADAMOPOULOS, D. A. and DOVE, G. A. (1970). *Br. med. J.* 3, 406.

DISCUSSION

In the discussion of endocrine influences on behaviour some apparently unanswerable questions were asked. To what extent can moral behaviour in man be understood in terms of biochemical and/or endocrine factors? The existence of externally induced mental abnormalities that mimic naturally occurring mental illnesses does not really help to answer this question. (These resemblances are extremely rare but amphetamine psychosis and acute paranoid schizophrenia present an almost exactly similar clinical picture.) The validity of the extrapolation of the results of experiments on laboratory animals to the clinical situation in man is always difficult to assess, and this problem is even more complex in the case of changes in behaviour or mood. Are there any reliable indices of mood changes in the lower animals? Extreme running activity in the rat (for example) may correspond to mania in man but it is difficult to confirm or refute comparisons scientifically. Cooperation between clinicians (for example psychiatrists and endocrinologists) and specialists in the physical sciences (biophysicists and biochemists) is poor, and too-early specialization inhibits this cooperation. The participation of biochemists and endocrinologists in the work in mental hospitals should be encouraged. Conversely, a psychiatrist is a most useful member of a general medical team.

Organic and functional factors are often combined in a single disease and treatment of either part of the disease may initiate cure. Anorexia nervosa is a particularly good illustration of this. The patient may improve psychologically as well as nutritionally if her starvation is tackled through hospitalization which ensures that she really is getting her diet, through intragastric tube feeding if necessary. But she may also regain her weight, appetite and menstrual periods through a dynamic psychotherapeutic exploration of her problems. Either method may break the vicious circle but a combination of the two is usually needed.

The oral contraceptive pill. Rapid and massive assimilation of the results of field studies on oral contraception has occurred, but appropriate questions may not have been asked nor suitable ways of defining the problems adequately thought out. The long-term effects of the pill are especially difficult to assess because so many different factors—medical, endocrine, social and psychological—are involved. Women may use different sorts of contraceptives on different occasions (for example, the pill for a regular partnership, local contraceptives for casual intercourse). In Western and many other cultures, feelings and *mores* about contraception are constantly changing; this adds to the difficulties of assessment.

4: Sex Offenders in Denmark

GEORG K. STÜRUP

SEXUAL crimes always have some relationship to the sex drives; besides this, the features common to all sexual crimes are of a legal character.

SEXUAL OFFENCES IN DENMARK

In Denmark, sexual offences are set forth in *The Danish Criminal Code*.[3] Persons who break the law by their sexual behaviour do not always have any sexual pathology and, conversely, sexual pathology is not identical with sexual crime.

Since 1933, homosexuality between adults, fornication, prostitution and sexual relations with animals are no longer punishable by law. In Chapter 24 of this Code, the most important offences are: section 216: rape; section 222: intercourse with any child under 15 years of age; section 225: acts of sexual immorality with a person of the same sex under 18 years of age. The most frequently used section—232—cites any person who by obscene behaviour violates public decency or gives public offence.

A great deal of difference exists between the various sex offences but they have one thing in common, namely, that the percentage of sex crimes solved is substantially higher than the percentage of crimes in general solved (Table I). The number of criminals, both sexual and other, sentenced each year in Denmark has been relatively constant during the nineteen-sixties. The number of first offenders convicted of a sex offence has varied from 307 to 351 and of recidivists from 180 to 230 each year. The number of recidivists has always been fewer than the number of first offenders.

Rate of recidivism

Very few sexual criminals recidivate with a new (that is, another) sexual crime. Moreover, the recidivism rate for sex offenders is much lower than it is for property offenders. We recently analysed the recidivism rate of 2934 sexual criminals sentenced during a ten-year period.[2] The recidivism rate was 24·3 per cent but this includes offences of all kinds. If we count only recidivism of new sexual crimes, the rate is only about 10 per cent.

A more detailed analysis revealed that first offenders had a recidivism rate of only 6·9 per cent for new sexual offences, while persons with a previous history of recidivism now recidivated at a rate of 23 per cent for

25

new sexual offences. On the other hand, persons whose previous history consisted of mixed property and sexual offences recidivated at a rate of 25 per cent for new sex offences and had a total recidivism rate of 45 per cent. Similarly, persons whose prior history had included only property offences had a sex offence recidivism rate of 9·7 per cent, that is, their sexual recidivism rate was slightly higher than that of first-time sexual offenders. Of special significance was the finding that the probability of committing a new sex offence seemed to be independent of age, provided that the groups at both extremes of the age continuum were excluded.

TABLE I

PERCENTAGE OF TOTAL AND SEXUAL CRIMES*
DETECTED, WITH ARREST, IN DENMARK IN 1964

Number, and percentage (in parentheses), of offences known to the police	Total	Sexual
	150 187 (100·0)	3681 (100·0)
Detected, with arrest	45 637 (30·4)	2093 (56·9)
Charges dropped for lack of proof, but probably detected	3746 (2·4)	464 (12·8)
Total offences probably detected	49 383 (32·8)	2557 (69·7)
Offences remaining undetected	100 804 (67·2)	1124 (30·3)

*Table I derived from Table 1, *Kriminalstatistik 1964*.[6] Sexual crimes include incest (122), rape (259), heterosexual indecency (2940) and homosexual indecency (364).

The likelihood of recidivating to the same kind of sexual offence is greatest in the case of those forms of sexual behaviour which are considered the most deviant from a strictly psychiatric point of view, namely, indecency towards children and exhibitionism. It is important, however, to distinguish between what may be deviant from a psychiatric point of view and what is most serious in its social consequences. These are by no means identical concepts.

Speaking more generally about our ten-year sample of sex offenders, we found that at least two types of sexual criminality were presented: (a) a group consisting largely of younger sex offenders whose criminal conduct was, presumably, for the most part, a symptom of puberty; and (b) a group of somewhat older sex offenders whose criminal conduct was, to a greater degree, the result of more deeply rooted tendencies. In the case of the younger group the prognosis was extremely favourable in regard to recidivism to new sexual crimes. Nevertheless, if we take a long-range perspective, we find that the probability of coming to the attention of the authorities for a new sex offence does not diminish with increasing age, it simply remains constant for a number of years. These facts about the long-range perspective make it difficult to evaluate sexual criminal careers and emphasize the necessity for using long periods of time in follow-up studies. This is essential in all aspects of research and treatment related to sex offenders.

26

Treatment considerations

From a treatment point of view it is important to distinguish between two types of behaviour: (*a*) the one-time, situationally conditioned, sexual behaviour of a criminal kind that has an especially good prognosis; and (*b*) the sexual behaviour of a criminal kind that is phenomenologically fully analogous to the first sort of behaviour, but which is really of a persistent character, despite an earlier legal admonishment (with or without an actual penal sentence), and carries with it a prognosis of increasingly frequent violations of the same nature. In the kind of out-patient work carried on in many places offenders of the first type are predominantly the subject of treatment; by contrast, in the detention institution at Herstedvester, offenders in the second group predominate.

On the basis of previous Scandinavian experience, it has been stressed[15] that most sex offenders feel a great need for treatment. They require help in coping with an experience that seems to overwhelm them almost against their will. The ethical insight of these inmates is usually quite clear and when one penetrates their protective shell they are found to be full of self-reproach which has interfered with the process of free communication. Even if special psychiatric treatment were not to result in statistically lower rates of relapse—it probably would but it would be difficult to demonstrate—such treatment has an independent humanitarian value. In most cases, however, supportive treatment is sufficient provided that it is carried out in an objective atmosphere.

It is also necessary to make a realistic evaluation of the practical, real-life possibilities for the future careers of these inmates. In some cases supportive therapy will reveal special problems that may need more radical treatment, usually of an in-depth, analytic, casework type. Stilboestrol has been used with effect in selected cases of transsexualism and in subjects who were psychologically disturbed by compulsive masturbation. Breast enlargement was a common side effect, often welcomed by the transsexual patient but an annoyance for the others. Stilboestrol has only been useful for a few of our selected group of sexual criminals, but some of them have preferred it to any other treatment. An antihormone such as cyproterone acetate may be of practical value. In a very few cases castration has been desired by the detainee and found to be the most reasonable therapeutic measure. In such cases supportive psychotherapy has been used before operation to verify this decision on the part of the detainee and then to support it.

Castration

Due to the existence of a special castration law in Denmark we have had the opportunity of advising some of our offenders that they may apply for a permit to be castrated. Thus, in addition to the general course of treatment described above, we also have this special opportunity to assist these very unfortunate human beings so that they may be able to avoid sex crimes in the future.

Denmark has been a pioneer in this field of legislation although castration had been resorted to in earlier times and at other places. As early as 1892, Forel castrated a hypersexual patient and achieved a favourable result. Similarly, in 1906, Oberholzer and von Suri in Switzerland each performed a castration for clearly forensic psychiatric reasons. More cases followed, and in the first quarter of the twentieth century Meyer[7,8] recommended that persons suffering from their sexual drives and attempting to resist their urges be operated on. Even today, in both Switzerland and Holland, castrations are performed without the basis of positive legislation, that is, they are performed on the basis of an interpretation of the laws related to mayhem. The earliest suggestions for legislation permitting sterilization and castration in Denmark were made in 1912 by Keller who worked in an institution for mental defectives.

It is necessary that sterilization and castration be distinguished, for they are not the same. The object of sterilization is simply to achieve infertility. In castration the testes are removed and the production of sex hormones ceases.* In 1921 Danish women's organizations suggested a change in the criminal code designed to protect society against recidivist rapists. In 1923 a committee reported on this matter and concluded that although castration could not be used as punishment, nor could it be used as a substitute for the punishment of a crime, there might very well be humanitarian reasons to permit surgical intervention for those persons who requested it because they felt unable to control their sexual urges and thus were liable to resort to criminal means to satisfy them. Since it was considered that such an operation could not be performed by a doctor without exposing him to the liability of a criminal charge (mayhem) if the operation were not strictly necessary on medical grounds, the committee decided to propose special enabling legislation that would permit such operations under proper safeguards.

A new committee was then appointed to make a more thorough study of the implications concerning sterilization and castration. In 1926 this committee produced a report proposing a special law. The draft produced by the new committee specified that persons over 21 years of age, on application, should be allowed to obtain a permit to be castrated, or to submit to other surgical intervention on their sexual organs, provided that their sexual drive, because of its abnormal strength or direction, placed them in danger of committing a crime and they thus represented a danger to themselves or society. In addition, this draft set forth conditions permitting intervention for sterilization in the case of certain

---

* The testes are usually replaced by protheses in order to keep the appearance of the scrotum unchanged.

mentally abnormal persons. In 1929, this law was accepted by Parliament and, since it was a typically experimental law, provisions were included that after a few years of operation the law should be reviewed for purposes of possible amendment. In addition to the provisions suggested by the draft, which have already been mentioned, the 1935 law* also included a provision for the forced castration of certain very serious sexual criminals. I hasten to add that no forced castration has ever been carried out in Denmark. Nevertheless, in the new law of 1967 only voluntary castration may be carried out.

Castration and recidivism

A brief account of the results of legal castration in Denmark has been published.[12] This is a study of 900 cases covering the thirty-year period 1929–1959. About one third of these were detainees in prison or prison-like institutions, 300 were patients in mental hospitals and institutions for mental defectives, and the remaining 300 were operated on following their own request, that is, they were not institutionalized. The minimum age (by law) for operation is 21 years. The age range in this series of 900 men was 24 to 68 years. This work is of special significance because the Danish law made follow-up studies conducted under the auspices of the Medico-Legal Council mandatory. Professor Knud Sand was head of this Council for many years.

Altogether some 4000 separate follow-up investigations were conducted on 900 individuals during this 30-year period. In some cases an individual who had been operated on was examined as frequently as sixteen times, but most cases were examined from one to five times. The psychiatric evaluation of these 900 individuals is shown in Table II.

These cases were under observation for many years. The most important general results can be stated as follows: asexualization was found in 97 per cent of the cases. Only 20 of the 900 sex offenders recidivated (2·2 per cent), but even this favourable result must be qualified by pointing out that only ten recidivated in such a way as to leave no doubt that they were 'real sexual recidivists' while the other ten are less clear and must be considered borderline cases. It is also important to indicate that more than 90 per cent of these persons were satisfied with the operation.

The most common side effects of castration have been the following: (a) periods of sweating have been really troublesome and prolonged in only a few cases, but mostly sweating was of little consequence; (b) increase in weight—the most feared complication—has been, for the most part, moderate and in a few cases the patients lost weight; (c) enlargement of the breasts has been found in some cases; and (d) muscular power, as measured by a dynamometer, has been retained. No spontaneous

* Law 176, Permission to Sterilize and Castrate, May 11, 1935. This law has now been superseded by Law 234, June 3, 1967.

fractures have been observed as a result of the lower calcium content of bone after castration. The much-feared psychological consequences of castration in adult men have not been observed. About 2 per cent in this

TABLE II

PSYCHIATRIC EVALUATION OF 900 CASES LEGALLY CASTRATED
BETWEEN 1929 AND 1959

Category	Percentage
Mental defective	44
Psychopath	25
Sexually abnormal	13
Borderline case	10
Psychotic	4
Miscellaneous	1
Unclassified	3
Total	100

series complained of loss of ambition. About 33 per cent of hetero-sexuals retained some sexual potency. There was no evidence of increased incidence of prostatic cancer. Sand's most recent report,[12] like the con-clusion he formed earlier,[11] is that the results are fully satisfactory. Sand has said ". . . that legal castration must be looked upon as the best social measure for, and treatment of, sexual criminals, and abnormal sexuals in general; most humane in relation to the single subject and most effec-tive from a criminal-therapeutic and social point of view." It must, however, be emphasized that this conclusion is valid only for that small group of sexual offenders in whom experience has demonstrated that their sexual urges are beyond their control, that they are likely to recidi-vate and that they suffer great anguish because they constitute a great risk for themselves and others.

From a criminological point of view, the results of Sand's study of 900 Danish cases are excellent in every respect and the Danish experience is in full accord with results obtained from studies conducted in other European countries. From a medical point of view competent observers are satisfied that the purposes of surgical intervention have been achieved (that is, there has been a decrease in the sexual drive, which is partially a suppression) and there has been no important physical or psychological damage. After these careful follow-up studies on men, and considering what we already know about the effects of removing the ovaries of women,[4] there should no longer be any reason to speculate about the effects of castration on men.

The main conclusion to be derived from all this material on castrated men whose subsequent sexual career has been studied for many years is that a person who has suffered acutely—to the point of despair—as a result of his sexual drive will, on castration, feel a great sense of relief when he is freed from these fearful urges. This is in marked contrast to what may happen to a man who usually, if not always, has enjoyed the consequences of his sexual drive. In more technical and specific terms, the main effect of castration on men with serious sexual difficulties is that their sexual reaction, that is, their capacity to respond to sexual stimuli, is especially affected, as is their sexual fantasy life and their sexual interests in general. These results are emphasized by Bremer[1] who was the most sceptical of those who conducted follow-up studies. He concluded: "As long as a better medical treatment is not available, the operation should not be withheld from those exceptional cases who, after being carefully advised, choose this opportunity to be relieved of their suffering."

HERSTEDVESTER DETENTION CENTRE

Sand's first follow-up study on castration[11] was already available before I took up my position at Herstedvester. Nevertheless, both I and a number of my assistants who came later felt a sense of uneasiness about the use of the castration law. But as clinical experience accumulated it soon became apparent that resort to such a procedure was a great advantage, particularly in the situation in which we found ourselves and with the problems we faced. In contrast to other countries that lacked such legislation we had a real opportunity to help a group of people with special problems. In most other countries long terms of imprisonment for sex offenders are considered both necessary and reasonable, but such measures constitute a very serious intervention if we evaluate the effects of protracted institutionalization on the personality. On the other hand, whether we like it or not, it is a fact that the victims and relatives of sex offenders, as well as the public at large, usually demand such punishment, especially for the more sensational sex crimes.[14] Such feelings of retribution are quite independent of the fact that the very same persons may later recognize the necessity of a more treatment-oriented reaction.

A man who has committed one of the more serious sex offences, especially that small group of offenders who have repeated such attacks against women or children, as a rule experiences his deed as something dreadful, as something which overwhelmed him and which he is afraid he might repeat. We are referring to that small group of serious sexual offenders who are recidivists and whom we have seen at Herstedvester. Ordinarily they show signs of such fears and anxieties even when they do not admit their existence. Sometimes such an admission is made for the first time after they have been castrated and thus relieved of their fears. Only then can it be admitted that these were a hard burden to bear. In cases in whom symptoms of anxiety and fear are evident, whether admitted or not, a thorough examination of the man's entire biological history is conducted. Special emphasis is placed on his sexual development and state of anxiety. If the man's own fear of committing a new sex offence is well established, and if such a possibility is considered likely, then the opportunity of gaining relief through castration is mentioned and the advantages and disadvantages of this are fully discussed. The man must be given time to consider his decision, although it is quite likely that he had already made up his mind before he ever arrived at Herstedvester. Castration as a treatment method is now so well known in Denmark that he will have had occasion to discuss it before, either during a former imprisonment or during the course of a psychiatric interview. It is not unusual for a defence lawyer to broach the question. On reaching his decision the man himself files an application for castration and this is forwarded to the Ministry of Justice together with a full case history and psychiatric evaluation. All these materials are further evaluated by the Medico-Legal Council in its advisory capacity to the Ministry. The operation is carried out by a surgeon especially authorized to perform it. The patient stays in bed a few days and, in ordinary circumstances, is released from the hospital to the open section of Herstedvester 10 to 14 days after the operation.

Results of the castration programme at Herstedvester

The results of castration have been highly satisfactory from every point of view, including the psychiatric. This is largely because the operation is an integral part of a total treatment plan. Castration has never been advised unless, all things considered, the operation has been found to be clearly indicated from a medical point of view. It is designed to make life more bearable, by freeing a man from the fear of relapse and thus increasing his chances for a better future. This is not to say that life as a castrate is always happy. Life can be full of hardship and, when times of adversity come, the temptation can be great to blame the operation for one's misfortune. This is true not only of the castrate but also of outside observers who are not well informed. But once a period of adversity has been overcome the same persons may attribute their good fortune to the operation: this is just as unwarranted as the tendency to blame it.

It must be emphasized that castration is a serious form of intervention into the life of a man and, while I would not want to overstress the fact, it is true that some castrates commit suicide. In a group of 199 sex offenders who had been treated during the period 1935 to 1948, we found that by 1953 five had died by suicide. In none of these cases, however, was it possible to determine that castration had been the decisive factor. It must also be pointed out that suicide rates among criminal groups are higher than in the population at large.

During the period 1935 to 1965 a total of 368 sex offenders were received at Herstedvester on first sentence. They were not necessarily first offenders. Most had had previous convictions and many had previously committed sex offences. The distribution of these 368 sex offenders by type of offence, classification of victim and period during which they were received is shown in Table III.

TABLE III

TOTAL NUMBER OF SEX OFFENDERS TREATED AT HERSTEDVESTER,
1935–1965

Offence and victim	1935–1948	1949–1965	Total
Rape—adult woman	20	18	38
Sex offence—female child under 15 years of age	55	61	116
Sex offence—male child under 18 years of age	75	63	138
Sex offence—children of both sexes	29	9	38
Other—incest, exhibitionism, indecency	20	18	38
Total	199	169	368

Thirty-eight rapists received at Herstedvester, 1935–1961

Since our knowledge of criminal sexual careers is as limited as it is, I shall select a certain type of sex offender in order to illustrate some aspects of such careers and their final outcome. Since rape is considered to be the most serious of sex offences, from the point of view both of the general public and of the non-psychiatric rapist himself, we shall concentrate our attention on all the rapists received at Herstedvester during the period 1935 to 1961—a total of 38 cases. This group of offenders is sufficiently small to enable us to present some aspects of clinical analysis for an unbroken series of cases and to give some statistical information on the career and outcome of the entire group. It should be noted that only 18 of these 38 rapists were treated by castration. Some summary information about all these offenders is shown in Table IV. The 38 cases represent the major part of the most serious rape cases perpetrated in Denmark over a long period. A few cases of equal seriousness may have been sentenced to regular imprisonment during this time.

It is difficult to give a comprehensive overview of all this material but we will attempt a few generalizations. For convenience I have divided the time of study into two periods, 1935–1948 and 1948–1961. I shall refer to the former period as 'early' and the latter as 'late'. There were 20 men in the former and 18 in the latter period. In the early period 15 out of the 16 men who had raped adult women came from a rural environment with the remaining man coming from a provincial town. Of the eleven rapists in the late group, whose victims were also adult women, five were from Copenhagen, four from rural areas and two from provincial towns.

33

There were eleven paedophiliacs, four in the early and seven in the late group. Seven of these came from rural areas, one from a provincial town and three from the capital. These changes in place of origin probably reflect changes in the jurisdictional area where the offenders we receive are apprehended and processed, for, since October 1, 1952, we receive

TABLE IV

TOTAL NUMBER OF RAPISTS TREATED AT HERSTEDVESTER,
1935–1961

| Age of rapist at intake (years) | Type of victim | | |
	Adult	Female child under 15 years	Total
Under 20	1	0	1
20–29	13	4	17
30–39	9	4	13
40–49	1	3	4
Over 50	3	0	3
Total	27	11	38

only half of all the persons sentenced to detention, those from the eastern part of Denmark. These changes may also be related to a change in the nature of our client population in the direction of a greater proportion of psychopathological cases. For the most part rape has been a rural offence but as our jurisdiction shifts to a more urbanized area we tend to receive more psychopathological cases. While such subjects are more appropriate for hospitalization than for detention by law, it is unfortunate but true that there is a tendency to send them to us. After a period of time at Herstedvester we have been able to transfer several cases to mental hospitals.

In most of the cases the victims, whether adults or children, were unknown to the offender. This was especially true in the early period during which only two of the victims were previously known to the rapist, while 24 were unknown. However, five of these 24 unknown victims can be said to have been especially sought out. Similarly, in the late period, seven of the victims were previously known and 21 were unknown, but five of the latter were especially sought out. This category of victim, 'unknown but especially sought out', refers to victims who, although they are not personally known to the rapist, have some special quality about them that is peculiarly attractive to him. This quality may relate to their age, appearance, personal habits or ready accessibility as victims, and distinguishes them from those victims encountered by chance, at an opportune time, in a suitable situation. There may be some important differences among rapists based on this classification of victims but we are not yet ready to speculate about this.

On the basis of our data derived from the 38 rapists we could not confirm the hypothesis[10] that the careers of rapists demonstrate a progression from the milder forms of sexual deviation to the more serious ones. We are unable to affirm that sex offenders pass through increasingly serious stages, for example from pornography to peeping, to fetishism, to child molestation and then to rape. Some sexual criminals commit rape as their first offence and then go on to commit less serious offences. However, we must re-emphasize that sexual recidivism is an extremely rare phenomenon.

Rapists cannot clearly be classified on the basis of the kind of victims they choose to attack. Some rapists attack both adult and juvenile females. What can be asserted is that rapists may be classified on the basis not of an absolute but of a more or less dominant interest in a particular type of victim. The problem is to some extent situational. Thus, there is one group whose victims are mainly adult women, a second group whose victims are mainly children and a third smaller group whose victims are mainly older women.

The relationship of the use of alcohol to rape has some importance but should not be over-emphasized. Alcohol played a part in some of the offences, but in others, committed by both castrated and non-castrated men who drank to excess from time to time in the course of their parole periods, it did not lead to sexual recidivism. Heavy drinking was the decisive factor in the rapes committed by three of the 38 subjects. In these cases, however, alcohol seemed to release aggressive tendencies and the fact that they took a sexual direction was, more or less, accidental. One of these three subjects, who did not usually drink, got drunk the night after his wife had borne him a child. Another drank when he was feeling suicidal. In one paedophilic subject the rapes were clearly the result of excessive drinking. When he became drunk his capacity for being sexually stimulated by young girls seemed to be easily aroused. When he was sober he had great difficulty in recognizing these tendencies in himself.

It has been maintained that the persistent rapist does not exist.[9] Our data show that although such cases are rare they do occur. There were five in this series of 38 cases. One example from these five is a primitive and impulsive man who, at the age of 25 years, attempted to rape a girl of 20. He was sent to prison for 18 months and then served several additional terms for property offences. Shortly after his release from the last of these he raped a 55-year-old widow. This time he was sent to prison for eight years. Upon release he again raped a girl of 20 years of age and this is the offence that resulted in his detention at Herstedvester. Of the other four persistent rapists, three were known to have committed twelve rapes against women aged between 48 and 85 years during a four-year period. From a psychiatric point of view these five cases do not resemble each other. Two are similar with respect to their primitivism, dullness and impulsiveness, but otherwise they are very different kinds of persons: one is emotionally labile and the other more schizoid and paranoid. The other three are also very different psychiatrically. One is self-assertive and dominating, the second is explosive and hysterical, and the last suffers from syphilitic locomotor ataxia and relative impotence so that only strong aggressive emotions can produce ejaculation.

Further attempts at a psychiatric classification of the non-persistent rapists did not result in any clearly defined sub-groups. They are an extremely heterogeneous group of persons. The non-psychotic castrates who are interested in adults as sexual objects cannot be psychiatrically distinguished from the paedophiliacs. Even the three gerontophiliacs have no other traits in common.

It can be said that nearly all these men have an easily aroused sex drive; they suffer from some sort of sexual hyperaesthesia. To say this, however, is to do no more than to give a name which may not have been particularly obvious to a presumed predisposition to rape. Many of our cases may be described as being sensitive but this is not a general characteristic. The notion that rapists are characterized by an augmented libido figured rather prominently in the diagnoses we made at first, but more mature reflection made us realize that the quantity of libido is very difficult to measure. The investigator is completely dependent upon the testimony of the person being examined and several cases have come to our attention where no claims to an increased libido were made. Sadistic elements may be present in these cases but, contrary to what is often maintained, we did not commonly find this. Unless such elements are part of a psychotic syndrome it seems that sadism and, for example, paedophilic tendencies are not particularly related.

It may well be asked why earlier research in this area has not resulted in the same negative findings as those that I have emphasized here, and the answer may be that such evaluations were attempted under very different conditions. The period of psychiatric observation has been relatively short in many studies which have usually been conducted in connexion with court hearings. Earlier research has not been based on many years of continuous observation focusing on the total careers of the offender both inside an institution and in the free community. Such a long-term perspective is essential for obtaining the true psychiatric picture. From a therapeutic point of view it is not as important to attempt to make an evaluation of the absolute strength of the libido as it is to arrive at an informed estimate of the relative strength of a set of personality variables that include: (a) the strength of libido; (b) the intensity of the stimuli the man might encounter; (c) the manner in which he perceives the relationship; and (d) the general forces of resistance he can muster. The cases where these elements are seriously out of balance are especially unfortunate. The likelihood of recidivism is great in those cases where the personality is weak and insecure, where intellectual handicaps limit the degree of personality development possible and especially in cases with a previous history of serious sexual offences. In such cases castration has been advised and the results have been good.

In men with serious psychiatric problems (for example schizophrenia) the operation is not indicated. It also seems sensible not to operate on such persons in order to avoid discrediting a good treatment method through failings not particularly related to it. Social therapy combined with a relatively superficial form of psychotherapy is the most effective treatment for psychopaths. This has been our method of growth therapy, and others[5,13] agree that this is sufficient.

Hyatt Williams[16] finds such treatment 'useless' for sexual murderers. But he stresses that it is necessary to give these patients a 'second chance of taming the savage internal figures . . . This can be achieved only by a methodical and patient working through, in the transference, of the early situations with the bringing into the doctor-patient relationship the primitive, savage part of the murderer.' (p. 375). This does not accord with our experience. It is of course true that very few rapists are also murderers, but our experience with a whole series of homicidal offenders indicates that they are not very different from the group of rapists we have been discussing. Certainly the type of person sentenced to detention or imprisoned for life for sexual murder does not differ psychologically from the homicidal offender. Secondary reactions such as depression, amnesia or lack of affect are pronounced in both types of case but these can be overcome after a time. If our kind of therapy is successfully carried out and followed-up in the ambulatory phase, it is certain that the risk of recidivism would be minimal. Further, it is not likely that most of our cases would have been able to resolve their infantile traumas through depth treatment, because of their personality deviations and primitiveness.

From the standpoint of crime prophylaxis the results of our treatment methods are very satisfactory. No rapist who has been treated at Herstedvester has ever been returned for rape. There are two cases with no previous conviction for a sexual offence, both of whom were strictly property offenders, who committed rape after leaving Herstedvester, but these are not among the 38 rapists in this series.

After reviewing these cases, one is left with a very strong impression of a great discrepancy between the way in which these persons are described shortly after their offence and during the earliest stage in the institution compared with the impression one gains of their personality after contact of long duration and especially after resocialization. Resocialization has been achieved in most of the cases that have not developed a psychosis. The explanation for this discrepancy is no doubt complicated and multifactorial. The situation has changed and there may have been personality growth depending on a long series of unknown circumstances. The essential ingredient may even have been an erroneous evaluation of the personality at the time of the original investigation.

If we bear in mind the great variety of factors that have entered into the life careers of the sex offenders we have been discussing, both before they came to Herstedvester and in their post-institutional lives, it is easier to understand how difficult it really is to generalize about them. In many cases the degree of sensitivity exhibited by the offender may have been great and his own 'negative' reaction to his experience of the offence must be taken into consideration as an essential element in his future career. What would it have meant, for example, if someone had taken the initiative and related himself to the man in a meaningful way so that he would have received understanding at a crucial moment? What would it have meant if the most useful therapeutic occasions had been seized upon at precisely the right moment? I am afraid we know too little about these matters. In most of the 38 cases I have been describing such therapeutically useful situations have arisen repeatedly over the years. They must be exploited to full advantage in those for whom castration is appropriate and in those for whom it is not, for most sexual offenders are persons in great need of help.

Should sexual criminals be treated separately from other offenders? I do not think so. Such a separation would serve to aggravate the degree of self-depreciation which is the result of the general public's attitude toward sex offenders, shared for the most part by the sex offenders themselves. It is important from a therapeutic point of view that we have the possibility of giving special assistance to a certain number of cases through castration. In these selected cases, castration can serve to limit the urges which had previously led to misfortune for lack of control. And although we may assist only a small minority of sexual offenders in this way it is helpful to treat them together with other types of offenders who are in need of specialized assistance. Any artificial separating out of sexual offenders from others may have negative therapeutic consequences that may complicate our task.

CONCLUSIONS

I would like once more to emphasize my personal dislike of the idea of castration imposed as a penal measure. I believe this operation to be beneficial, when accepted voluntarily, to certain types of offender but I regard it as a clinically therapeutic measure rather than as a means of protecting society. I find convincing the freedom from the terror of uncontrollable sexual impulses which it can give to suitable men.

REFERENCES

1. BREMER, J. (1965). *Tidsskr.norske.Laegeforen*. **85**, 384.
2. CHRISTIANSEN, K. O., NIELSEN, E., LE MAIRE, L. and STÜRUP, G. K. (1965). *Recidivism among Sexual Offenders*. In *Scandinavian Studies in Criminology*. Oslo: Universitetsforlaget.
3. DANISH CRIMINAL CODE (1958). Chap. 24. Copenhagen: Gad, C. E.
4. DE RIVER, J. P. (1958). In *Crime and the Sexual Psychopath*, p. 128. Springfield, Ill.: Thomas.
5. JENKINS, R. L. (1960). *J. nerv. ment. Dis*. **131**, 318.
6. KRIMINALSTATISTIK 1964 (1966). Copenhagen: Gad, C. E. (Official document of criminal statistics.)
7. MEYER, H. W. (1911). *Juridische-Psychiatrische Grenzfragen*. Bd. 8.
8. MEYER, H. W. (1925). *Z. Neurol*. **95**, 200.
9. PLAUT, P. (1960). In *Der Sexualverbrecher und seine Persönlichkeit*, p. 79. Stuttgart: Enke.
10. REINHART, J. M. (1957). In *Sex Perversions and Sex Crimes*, p. 16. Springfield, Ill.: Thomas.
11. SAND, K. (1940). *Nord. Med*. **6**, 779, 893, 1029.
12. SAND, K., DICKMEISS, P. and SCHWALBE-HANSEN, P. (1964). *Betaenkning om Sterilisation og Kastration*, **353**, 46–57.
13. SCOTT, P. (1964). In *The Pathology and Treatment of Sexual Deviations*, p. 104, ed. Rosen, J. London: Oxford University Press.
14. STÜRUP, G. K. (1953). *International Review of Criminal Policy*. New York: UN Dept of Social Affairs.
15. STÜRUP, G. K. (1960). *Sex Offenses: The Scandinavian Experience in Law and Contemporary Problems*. Durham, N. C.: Duke University Press.
16. WILLIAMS, A. HYATT (1964). In *The Pathology and Treatment of Sexual Deviations*, p. 375, ed. Rosen, J. London: Oxford University Press.

DISCUSSION*

CONSENT

The question of voluntary consent for castration was discussed. Dr Stürup agreed that, given the likelihood that release from detention would probably be earlier for certain offenders with castration than without it, there were inevitably some circumstantial pressures towards application for the operation. There are safeguards against these pressures. The offender has to apply, in writing, to the Minister of Justice, who has to ask for advice from the Medico-Legal Council. Three experienced

* Note added in proof. The sexual laws in Denmark were substantially changed in their application during the period 1967–1969 in relation to the abandonment of pornography. How much influence this pornography freedom has meant is difficult to estimate yet, but fewer sexual crimes have been reported in the past two years. Whether fewer such acts are actually performed is another question. The substantial fall in sexual offences in general, however, does not relate to rape. The number of rapes reported is unchanged. This may mean that the hardship of being a sexual offender will become less, and it seems in any case that the attitude of the population is already influencing the attitude of the sexual offender to himself.

psychiatrists are members of this Council. They review the application and accompanying recommendation from Herstedvester and on the basis of this information decide whether or not to authorize the operation. Dr Stürup himself would advise castration in detention only when he would similarly have advised a patient at liberty outside. About two-thirds of the men in detention to whom castration is offered accept it and one-third do not. For a person who is unable to give responsible consent, such as a classified imbecile with an IQ of, say, less than 70 (although the IQ is not necessarily the deciding factor) and with complicating personality disorders, further consent must be given by a guardian *ad hoc*. The wife's consent was not legally required as a condition of her husband's castration. She would be consulted by the clinician acting on behalf of the Minister of Justice and the Medico-Legal Council and her point of view taken into account, although not necessarily followed.

CASTRATION AND ENGLISH LAW

The two major considerations are the offence in common law of mayhem and the principle of necessity. A disease of the testis would justify the surgeon in removing it. But the principle of necessity applies normally only to the patient himself—a procedure is carried out to alleviate or prevent a worse harm to him. Could this principle be extended for the protection of a third party to whom, without the operation, he might do harm? Or could it be said that in harming the third party he was harming himself, not only by putting himself within danger of the law and so of punishment but also by frustrating himself through once more making a sexual attack—an action which he feels he should not allow himself to do and which is unacceptable to him? Another unanswered question was whether the principle of necessity could justifiably be stretched to cover the removal of an undiseased testis. Denmark is the only country in which the (undiseased) testis enjoys special protection at law in that there is a prescribed legal procedure governing permission to operate on it.

5: Effects of Temporal Lobectomy on Personality in Epilepsy

M. A. FALCONER

EPILEPSY arising in one or both temporal lobes probably affects one person per thousand in the British Isles. Most cases are controllable by drug therapy, and only a minority requires or is amenable to surgical treatment. However, temporal lobe epilepsy is more frequently associated with psychiatric disturbances than is epilepsy arising in any other part of the brain, and the variety of temporal lobe disturbances can be exceedingly diverse. Probably the majority of those epileptic patients who require institutional care suffer from temporal lobe epilepsy.

At the Guy's-Maudsley Neurosurgical Unit over 200 patients have now been operated on by a standardized technique whereby the resected lobe is removed in one piece, allowing detailed pathological examination. Whenever possible these patients have been followed up at regular intervals in order to ascertain the results as regards both relief of seizures and social adjustment. Subsequently these results have been correlated with the underlying pathological changes which we think are the cause of the epilepsy. We have come to learn that in order to evaluate an operation it is not sufficient to take into account the abolition or relief of seizures, which is the criterion usually adopted by those who have carried out therapeutic trials with the various anticonvulsant drugs, but that one must also assess the social and psychological consequences.

Recently my colleague, Dr David Taylor, and I have completed a survey of the results of operation in 100 consecutive English-speaking patients who had been operated on from 2 to 10 years earlier. Their selection for operation had depended upon the facts that they had epilepsy of psychomotor type, and often of *grand mal* type as well, which had not responded to drug therapy, that they had no clinical or neuroradiological evidence of a tumour or other progressive lesion, and that they had a spike-discharging focus on the electroencephalograph which was exclusively or predominantly localized to the anterior part of one temporal lobe. As regards other criteria, we did not exclude any patient for his mental state, except for gross retardation indicating widespread brain disease or damage. We thus had patients with a wide range of psychiatric abnormalities in our sample, but even so our criteria of selection, based largely on the electroencephalographic

41

findings, were so rigorous that the majority of patients referred to us for operation were turned down as unsuitable.

At the time of operation our notes included ample data on the social background and mental state of our patients as well as on the nature and frequency of the fits. In following-up the patients we ascertained not only from the patient but also usually from a relative or friend what had happened to the seizures, and also the social adjustment both before and after operation, as covered by the following seven areas of social functioning: (a) had the patient ever been institutionalized (for example, in an epileptic colony, prison or mental hospital); (b) domicile (whether living at home in appropriate surroundings, in lodgings or institutions, or vagrancy); (c) the quality of family relationships (discord, disharmony and so on); (d) the quality of non-family relationships (for example, ability to make relationships with others); (e) working ability; (f) sexual adjustment (adequacy, disinterest, perversion); and (g) use of leisure.

Details of the technique of scoring are now published.[1]

CASE MATERIAL

There were 63 males and 37 females in the series of 100 patients; nine of these were operated on between the ages of 10 and 15, 66 between the ages of 15 and 35, and 25 over the age of 35 years. In contrast, in 46 patients the onset of the disease was in the first decade of life, in 31 it was in the second decade, and only in 23 patients was it in later years. The proportions of right-sided and left-sided resections were approximately the same and the mean follow-up was 68 months. There was no operative mortality and negligible morbidity apart from the production of a slight alteration of vision (an upper-quadrantic homonymous hemianopia). All the patients with left-sided resections showed some degree of impairment of auditory memory and learning, but we have recently shown that this defect disappears within 3 to 5 years.

At the time of follow-up a personal interview took place in 84 cases; three cases were abroad, two untraceable and eleven had died. Five of the eleven had committed suicide, two died of status epilepticus and four of natural causes. In assessing what had happened to the 16 missed cases, who had been followed for periods of from 2 to 10 years, they were rated on the basis of data from their own doctors, relatives, or hospitals, or from our last annual interview. All the ratings were made by Dr Taylor, but the first five and last five were also rated independently by two other psychiatrists and their separate ratings were consistent with those of Dr Taylor.

As regards epilepsy, 42 patients had become completely seizure-free and a further 20 had had only an occasional seizure, making a success rate of 62 per cent. A further 22 patients had had their seizures reduced in frequency by at least 50 per cent, making a total improvement rate as regards seizures of 84 per cent.

The social background of most of these patients had previously been considerably disturbed. In 40 there was a family history of epilepsy or mental illness, 31 had been separated from at least one parent by illegitimacy, death or divorce, before the age of 15 years and 45 had been at some stage before operation in a colony or mental hospital, or in prison. At the time of follow-up, allowing for the fact that the 16 missed cases were assessed on the last available information, 61 had improved to some extent, 28 were much worse and 12 had deteriorated. Before operation only 13 patients were considered psychiatrically normal and 37 patients were unemployed. After operation the corresponding figures were 32 and 12 respectively.

Although, in general, relief or lessening of seizures was necessary for improvement in social adjustment, there were several exceptions. Thus an occasional patient might be relieved of seizures but still be incapacitated by his psychiatric state, particularly if it were a psychosis. Again, a few patients were benefited psychiatrically although their seizures continued. The ways in which the personality was most frequently improved were in reduction of the aggressive outbursts which are common in temporal lobe epilepsy. Next followed improvement in neurotic and depressive states, but improvement in psychotic states was rare.

The fields of social functioning in which improvements, when they did occur, were most often seen involved the choice of a more appropriate domicile, family and interpersonal relationships, and working ability. Improvements were seldom marked in sexual adjustment and in the use of leisure.

In a high proportion of patients a definite pathological lesion was found in the resected temporal lobe, the presence of the lesion being unsuspected before operation. Thus, in nearly half the cases, mesial temporal lobe sclerosis was encountered, in a fifth of the cases hamartomatous lesions of various types, in another fifth scars and infarcts which were obviously lesions acquired in later life, and in the remaining fifth no significant lesion was seen. It was of interest to us that our most favourable surgical results occurred when either mesial temporal sclerosis or a hamartoma was encountered, thus adding an in-built control to our surgical therapy.

CONCLUSIONS

In properly selected cases of drug-resistant temporal lobe epilepsy in which before operation the electroencephalographic abnormality is unilateral or predominantly unilateral, anterior temporal lobectomy is often efficacious not only in relieving epilepsy but also in improving the associated psychiatric disorders. It should be emphasized that surgery is not sufficient treatment by itself; help in social and psychological adjustment after the operation is also needed.

REFERENCE

1. TAYLOR, D. C. and FALCONER, M. A. (1968). *Br. J. Psychiat.* **114**, 1247.

6: Effects of Leucotomy on Personality

R. F. TREDGOLD

I HAVE been asked to discuss changes in personality resulting from leucotomy. This title suggests a fairly precise account, but if I am expected to give a clear scientific exposition of certain personality changes obviously due to certain cuts through the brain substance (though obviously not so intended by the surgeon) my paper will be a disappointment. The subject lacks both clarity and scientific assessment; it is surrounded by prejudice and wishful thinking. If we are to understand this we must go back to the early leucotomies, and not only to them but to still earlier ideas about the brain, magic and possession by devils, for the legacies of these are still with us.

These ideas must have influenced the reactions which greeted the first efforts at leucotomy (from which modern techniques have sprung) carried out in the nineteen-thirties by Almeido Lima, on the recommendation of Egas Moniz, in Portugal. Moniz had his own problems. The surgeon who takes up politics is unusual enough, but he did this with such success that he was a major figure in his country's delegation to the treaty of Versailles. Perhaps he saw the treaty's weaknesses as soon as and rather more constructively than Hitler did, for he went back to surgery, where he first designed cerebral angiography by thorium, itself a major advance, and then devised leucotomy for his many incurable and hopeless patients. This was not long after similar patients had been shown to benefit through equally brilliant ideas (with as little scientific basis) about convulsant drugs and electricity from Von Meduna in Hungary, Sakel in Vienna and Cerletti and Bini in Italy.

There is no doubt that Moniz and Lima had some success: tensions were reduced and behaviour improved, but at a cost—that of a deterioration of conceptual thought, of control and of consideration for others. Hence the operation aroused horror in doctors and was condemned by the clergy, Moniz being feared as one who could damage the soul.[3-5] It seems only fair here to emphasize the desperation which was felt by many doctors about the number of hopeless patients. Any measure, at almost any risk, seemed better than a prolonged living death for some 300–400 sub-human creatures, for whom each mental hospital doctor had to care. Without some of the courage and inspiration of these pioneers we should never have been able to develop the treatments we now have which have revolutionized the outlook for many patients. But we must also remember that there is still some desperation. We

45

have treatment, but not enough staff to provide it—an almost worse situation.

How much a doctor may risk on behalf of his patient is a problem that arises frequently in medicine, and in cases of mental illness it is often overloaded by two further difficulties. First, that the patient's judgment on the choice may be unobtainable or, if obtainable, impaired and, second, that the risk run consists of further damage to his personality, including his judgment. The extra burden of these risks has led some doctors to stress them—and adopt a policy of *laissez-faire*—on the principle of *primum non nocere*; (slipping into foreign tongues may be itself an escape from facing responsibility). But this position is illogical. To allow some diseases, for example schizophrenia and depression, to continue is to allow deterioration of personality; and the doctors' crime is equally grave, though one of omission. Surely we must agree then that to do nothing is to do harm. This concept is relevant to such widely different but equally controversial subjects as abortion, euthanasia, drug addiction and, indeed, education in its widest sense.

Let us go back to the attitude of the public in Portugal and elsewhere to Moniz's operation. Their dismay, fear or horror led to the development of an aura around the word leucotomy which still persists. Although many modifications have been made to retain the value of Moniz's cuts without the risk of damage, the operations in use now are as different from the original in their extent and location as an appendicectomy is from a cholecystectomy, and although to compare them is ridiculous, people still do so. Partly this is prejudice and partly it is because the term leucotomy is still used for all types of this operation.

The reaction against leucotomy is greatest in the United States, where the operation is practically obsolete. That this is not entirely due to scientific objectivity is shown by some violent American attacks on progress here. In the United Kingdom there seems little doubt that leucotomy is recommended mostly by psychiatrists from a few geographical areas, presumably because they know successful surgeons in their neighbourhood. The implication is that one must not rely on publications; one must know the surgeon personally.

The modification of this operation best known to me is the restricted orbital undercut, designed by Geoffrey Knight. I took part in a survey of 350 consecutive cases operated on by him (or by his colleagues, using his methods).[6] In the survey we collected a team consisting of a psychiatric social worker, a psychologist and a psychiatrist, and let each of them assess the changes which had occurred clinically and socially. In summary, we found that 80 per cent of the cases were improved (49 per cent of them enough to be out of medical care) and 62 per cent were working with little or no incapacity, whereas only 8 per cent had done so before operation. On the debit side, 5 patients (1·5 per cent) died, apparently from the operation, and 12 per cent developed transient epileptiform attacks.

Such results would be good for most treatments; here they occurred in a group of patients previously regarded as hopeless. But this is not the major topic of this paper.

We must now ask several questions about our results. Was there personality damage? If so, in how many patients? And why? And, finally, are the risks justifiable? I hope that an account of our answers to the first three questions, and the reasoning which led to them, may help us to answer the last question. In some cases there was, in our view, no sign of any damage. Many patients were happier, showed no loss of moral, intellectual or aesthetic standards and seemed to be their old selves, freed from a terrible illness. They returned to strenuous jobs, such as senior industrial executive positions or teaching, and have remained in them for years. One illustration was an old lady of over 70 years of age, who had been ill for years, but after operation returned home, married a widower with three children and took up again her old hobby of singing. Nothing in the operation, therefore, necessarily produced damage.

There were other cases in whom deterioration had perhaps occurred. This is not easy to measure. We set about it in various ways. Relatives were asked to describe *any* changes in the patient's feelings, his attitude to himself or others, or his behaviour. Twelve changes were recorded, the most significant being a reduction of standards, a release of hostility and a lack of consideration. Some behavioural change was reported in over 50 per cent of our series and in 49 patients there had been a reduction of standards. But surprisingly, many of these patients were in the group regarded as completely relieved and the change had been beneficial; for example, a paralysed obsessional patient became free and happy. If we agree that a conscience can be morbidly increased, then, surely, it is right and beneficial to reduce it by medicine, surgery or psychiatry. A release of hostility also seemed sometimes to have been beneficial, provided it was constructively expressed. To produce such a result, help was generally necessary.

No one of these changes was therefore in itself evidence of personality deterioration. But we felt that several changes together might be so. We studied their grouping. In 17 patients we found a constellation of factors and these patients were indeed less well clinically and socially. There were also 20 who were regarded by their relatives as being, on balance, worse than before the operation. Twelve patients were recognized as social problems. As there was some overlap between these three groups, they totalled altogether 32 patients. To these should be added 9 patients who were in hospital at the time of interview. So there was a total of 41 patients who might possibly have suffered adverse effects.

These 41 patients were studied singly, and were found to fall into five groups: (a) those whose previous illness could well have been responsible for deterioration (mostly schizophrenics); (b) those whose previous treatment—that is, another leucotomy—could have been responsible; (c) cases of grossly inadequate previous personality; (d) those who, although showing multiple behaviour changes, were regarded unanimously as better; and (e) those in whom deterioration appeared to be due to this operation.

Our results have been criticized as unscientific. For the results of a survey like this to be scientific a controlled experiment would be necessary. This would entail finding precisely similar cases, and exposing them to exactly similar treatment in every particular, except that no cut in brain substance would be made. Everything else, including trephining the skull, would be similar. Although some attempt at this has been made,[1,2] most of the subjects were psychotic and only very tentative conclusions could be drawn owing to the large number of variables. There are objections to such a plan, not only on grounds of professional ethics but also because it presupposes the discovery of exactly comparable patients in exactly comparable circumstances for the two series, a situation which would almost never arise. The lack of adequate controls in this sense must therefore be accepted. It has been suggested that the patients might have had a spontaneous remission without operation. It is impossible to deny this, but it must be said that such a possibility did not seem likely to the referring psychiatrists (remembering that their recommendations must be based on probabilities). It has also been suggested that the results of the operation do not depend on the cut, but on the psychotherapeutic influence of the personality of the surgeon, and of the nursing attention, interest in a follow-up and, in some depressives, the punishment wished for and felt to be provided by the operation.

These suggestions are stimulating—though they are unacceptable to me personally and to others in close contact with such patients—and they would be fascinating to follow up; for they would of course lead (if true) to the conclusion that a surgeon and his colleagues, all unassisted by an analytic training, had achieved literally a very short cut to remarkable clinical results by spending relatively few hours with a large number of patients. As these results compare favourably with those of a trained psychoanalyst spending much more time with fewer patients, such a conclusion would entail complete rethinking of the qualifications and training of any psychotherapist. Even if we reject this contention, I must state my own view that in some cases help from the latter environment, in particular family support and psychiatric treatment, is a necessary adjunct to the operation (as is further discussed below).

Finally, even if these results are attributable to the operation, it can still be asked if any other means of treatment would have been equally successful. No certain answer can be given to this question. Further modifications of surgery, and new drugs, are of course always under consideration, and a series of patients in whom the corticothalamic tracts have been interrupted by radioactive yttrium is currently being studied (G. Knight, personal communication).*

It should here be pointed out that relatively few patients in our series had had full-scale psychotherapy. Whether this would have been equally or more successful than operation is another unanswered question. But what can be said is that it is most unlikely that psychotherapy of the skill and intensity required will be available for many such cases in mental hospitals in the foreseeable future.

SUMMARY

1. This type of operation does not *necessarily* cause damage to personality.

2. On the contrary, it enables many patients to live a fuller life in every sense.

3. It allows some patients to feel and express repressed emotions which, if well handled, can lead to improvement (exactly what psychotherapy aims to do), but (without skilled help) this may lead to deterioration.

4. In a few patients, about 5 per cent, deterioration may occur as a result of the operation, and death is a risk in $1 \cdot 5$ per cent. This must be set against the benefits.

5. The responsibility for assessing these benefits lies with the patient's medical advisers after consultation with patient and relatives. This responsibility must include an assurance that psychotherapy, if later required, will be available.

6. We may hope that even these risks will be diminished with further progress in surgery, and results with radioactive yttrium are encouraging.

REFERENCES

1. METTLER, F. A. (ed.) (1949). *Selective Partial Ablation of the Frontal Cortex*. New York: Hoeber.

2. METTLER, F. A. (1952). *Psychosurgical Problems*. London: Routledge and Kegan Paul.

* Note added in proof by Dr Tredgold. The results of 150 cases treated by yttrium implant have now been published (1971. Ström-Olsen, R. and Carlisle, S. *Br. J. Psychiat.* **118**, 141) and on the whole are very similar to those obtained by the operation of restricted orbital undercut, quoted above; although more cases were unimproved, no fatalities and no adverse sequelae occurred.

3. Moniz, E. (1936). *Lisb. méd.* **13**, 141.
4. Moniz, E. (1936). *Encéphale* **31**, 1.
5. Moniz, E. and Lima, A. (1936). *Lisb. méd.* **13**, 152.
6. Sykes, M. K. and Tredgold, R. F. (1964). *Br. J. Psychiat.* **110**, 609.

DISCUSSION

EPILEPSY

Six persons per 1000 suffer from some form of epilepsy, a symptom occasioned by a sudden electrical discharge in the grey matter of the brain. This discharge is usually caused by a macroscopic or microscopic abnormality in the cortex. The form of the attack is determined by the site of origin and the force and extent of the discharge.

In its social aspects epilepsy—the sacred disease—is burdened with fears of loss of work, insanity and death. The suddenness of the rupture of consciousness, as well as being disturbing personally, imputes social and economic unreliability to the epileptic. This sudden 'death' can build up in the epileptic a sense of isolation from a society that cannot help him. The popular attitude is at variance with the medical facts and possibilities.

CONTROLS

We discussed some of the problems connected with the setting-up of appropriate control groups for assessing new treatments, in particular for operations on the brain. We also discussed some general ethical and legal problems connected with the need for obtaining controls for new treatments in human beings without thereby compromising human freedom; and we examined some of the difficulties encountered in obtaining consent without coercion for new or experimental treatments, especially in subjects who were not legally responsible.

Control groups for cerebral surgery

Selection of cases for operations on the brain (leucotomy and temporal lobectomy, for example) is difficult enough; finding matched controls so that patients can be allocated randomly into two groups is even more so. Attempts to match descriptions of leucotomy patients with descriptions of similar patients from other mental hospitals have not been successful. In some circumstances patients might be observed for some months before and then after leucotomy, thereby acting as their own controls. The idea that a control group could be 'treated' with some or all of the procedures associated with leucotomy but without actual division of nervous connexions is not as useful as it sounds (*v.i.*). Another possible way of establishing a comparable control group for patients undergoing leucotomy would be to compare them with a group of matched patients treated by another form of surgery (for example, interruption of the corticothalamic tracts by yttrium implants).

General ethical considerations

Is it unethical, without using controls, to administer treatment that has not been proved effective? Are even imperfect controls better than no controls? Treatments established without controls have sometimes been found to be useless (blood-letting for many different diseases) or even harmful (when chloramphenicol first became available it was given extensively to children with whooping cough before it was discovered that the drug can induce fatal aplastic anaemia). Is it ethical or legal to give an admittedly experimental but probably helpful treatment to one patient and withhold it from another? Would it be ethically justifiable to incise the scalp of a control subject and, if so, what liabilities might attach on the grounds of unnecessary assault or mutilation? Is it justifiable to anaesthetize control patients?

All these problems are particularly complex when a patient is not legally responsible (that is, unable to give or refuse consent). In these circumstances, and in the case of minors, consent must be obtained from the relatives. For drug trials in minors or those who cannot give voluntary consent, using a control group would probably only be considered justifiable if the control procedure is a real attempt at treatment, not just a dummy or placebo. An important aspect of the problem of setting-up controls for leucotomy seems, therefore, to be the decision as to whether an operation, and associated preoperative and postoperative care without actual division of nervous tissue, might be regarded as, potentially, a treatment. Viewed in this way the experiment would be with two alternative methods of treatment, both covered by the principle of necessity, not with one method only, which is tested by means of a control. In these circumstances the patient could also be his own control: if the control treatment were seen not to have succeeded, the new treatment could be used later.

The essence of controls is that they are selected on a random basis and, in the case of leucotomy, neither the surgeon who does the operation, nor the nursing and all other personnel concerned with the patient, nor the patient himself should know who has had the active treatment and who has not. The only way in which a leucotomy operation can be controlled is by comparing it with another operative technique. If a definitive operation is performed in one group it must also be performed in the other. Thus, giving an anaesthetic and incising the scalp does not make an adequate control because the surgeon and nursing staff know the difference between this procedure and leucotomy. The patient soon gets to know whether he has had an operation or a dummy run.

Legal considerations

There are, not surprisingly, different national attitudes to leucotomy. Leucotomy is approved of in Portugal (Roman Catholic) and disapproved of in both Spain (Roman Catholic), and the USSR (communist) where leucotomy is regarded as an assault on the person. As far as criminal law in the United Kingdom is concerned, the legal position about experimental treatment of a therapeutic nature hinges on the following issues: (*a*) the acceptance of the experimental treatment in reputable medical circles; if it has not been so accepted the burden of proving its efficacy in the particular circumstances is much heavier. If a patient in the control group dies this could amount to manslaughter but under proper conditions would be very unlikely to be so regarded; (*b*) the consent given by the patient and, if possible, his close relatives—there must be no coercion; and (*c*) if the operation is a surgical necessity in the circumstances. This would be a particularly important issue for an unconscious or mentally disturbed patient, and in an emergency.

Civil liability in tort would not presumably arise if consent had been given and the necessary caution observed in performing the operation. In both civil and criminal cases the consent to the operation would be conditioned by the contract entered into by the patient, namely, whether the agreement was to a specific operation (for example, leucotomy) or to such other treatment as seemed necessary when the patient was anaesthetized.

---

* Note added by Mr Falconer after the meeting. Not all members of the group were in agreement with this view. It was suggested that the argument could be met if surgeon and theatre staff told no one which patient was which.

7: Psychoanalysis and the Schizophrenias

THOMAS FREEMAN

It is never easy to dispense with theory in the presentation of a psychoanalytic topic because concepts which comprise the different theories within psychoanalysis are essential for both the description and explanation of the signs and symptoms of a particular mental illness. In this paper I shall try both to avoid those theoretical ideas which are distant from clinical observations and also to ensure that concepts are not treated as if they were objective facts.

The concept of schizophrenia

Psychiatrists are entirely dependent on their examination of the patient when making their assessment of his mental state. This assessment cannot be checked by the independent and reasonably objective examinations provided by biochemists, pathologists and radiologists. Subjective factors in the psychiatrist play a much greater part in his evaluation of the mental disorder than occurs with a physician in the case of a physical illness. It is difficult, therefore, for psychiatrists to agree consistently about diagnosis and about what constitutes schizophrenia, manic depression or paranoia. The result is an inexact system of classification of mental illness.

Both in this country and abroad psychiatrists differ over what clinical states should be included within the nosological entity 'schizophrenia'. Some authors,[1] reverting to the views of Kraepelin, the founder of contemporary psychiatric classification, regard schizophrenia as a specific variety of mental illness which begins in adolescence or early adult life and is characterized by a progressive decline of intellect and emotion. Only rarely is there complete recovery. An opposite view is taken by other psychiatrists,[2] who consider that more than one variety of schizophrenia exists. They suggest that there are a number of mental illnesses occurring at all ages, the manifestations of which are sufficiently alike to allow them to be brought together as a group of schizophrenias. According to this approach patients suffering from one or other type of schizophrenia may recover spontaneously or with the help of treatment. These differences in opinion have led to much confusion because no one knows precisely what kinds of illness are being investigated.

The clinical observations which will be presented in this paper are drawn from a series of patients whose illness began between the ages

53

of 15 and 22 years. In every case the condition entered a chronic state after one or more remission of symptoms. These cases would be regarded by all psychiatrists as schizophrenic.

It is no accident that thus far the term disease has been conspicuous by its absence. This is because psychiatrists differ in their conception of mental illness. For some, mental illness is the result of physical disease; for others, it is the expression of an inability to adapt to the demands of life.

How does psychoanalysis stand in these matters? In its origins[4] psychoanalysis sought explanations no different from those looked for by the nineteenth-century advocates of the brain disease theory of mental illness. Freud, influenced by his background of anatomy and neurology, tried to accommodate what he observed to the mechanistic model of disease. It was only after several years experience with patients suffering from mental disorders that he arrived at the conclusion, which others were to reach later, that mental events cannot be satisfactorily explained in terms of brain dysfunction.

Before his inquiries into mental illness Freud,[3] influenced by the writings of Hughlings Jackson, had rejected the theory that mental functions (for example speech) could be localized to a specific region of the brain. This reluctance to accept a point-to-point correspondence between brain function and mental activity possibly allowed Freud to turn away more easily from the brain disease theory of mental illness. He then proceeded to elaborate a purely psychological theory, divorced from brain pathology, which postulated that mental symptoms were the outcome of alterations in the mental functions themselves.

Clinical manifestations of schizophrenia

The symptoms of a schizophrenic illness can be divided into two main groups: first, those which represent a loss or disturbance of mental faculties and, second, those which are foreign to the mentally healthy and detract from the task of adaptation to the environment. Sometimes these categories are described as negative and positive symptom groups. Typical of the former are loss of interest in others, a loss of the capacity for fluent speech and thinking, disturbances in the initiation of voluntary movements, and a general lack of responsiveness. Characteristic of the latter are new modes of thinking, irrational ideas (delusions) and false perceptions (hallucinations).

The psychoanalytic approach to the patient who presents such symptoms is a practical one. The psychoanalytic psychiatrist is not concerned with the question of whether or not the symptoms are the direct expression of brain disease. He wants to find out what purpose the symptoms serve, what is their meaning, why they came into being and, above all, what kind of person it is that has fallen ill. When these questions are satisfactorily answered it is possible to come to some conclusions regarding the further course of the illness and the treatment and management of the patient.

The information which the psychoanalyst seeks is often difficult to obtain because the patient suffering from schizophrenia differs from other sick persons in that he has lost the desire or the ability to communicate verbally with others. When approached he may ignore the friendly overture. He may be completely inaccessible. If addressed by name he may turn away or if he answers his lips may move but no sounds emerge. The disinterest may be less and he may answer questions but, after a short while, will bring the meeting to an end. There are other patients who talk freely during their first meetings with a psychiatrist and then refuse further communication.

Although some patients are withdrawn and self-preoccupied from the beginning of the illness there are others who give the psychiatrist the opportunity to hear about their experiences. At this time the patient may be extremely apprehensive and in a state of mental turmoil. He may ask all kinds of questions, revealing his own preoccupations, as if trying to find some reason for his strange experiences. As the illness passes into a more chronic state, the withdrawal and detachment tend to become more pronounced. The disinterest is not confined to others but applies equally to the self—hence the patient looks unkempt, dirty and neglected.

Close observation of patients, even those who are inaccessible to the psychiatrist, shows that they have by no means broken off all contact with the world around them. A case in point is that of a young, single man of 20 years of age who, after admission to hospital, avoided the company of other patients and staff. He refused to speak to the writer. His one expressed thought was the wish to leave the hospital. The only trace of interest in another person appeared when an occupational therapist came to see him suggesting that they might work together. The few remarks the patient made to her showed that he was uncertain about her identity. As the weeks passed he became very attached to her. He attended the occupational therapy centre. During these meetings the occupational therapist was sometimes able to help him overcome the sudden appearance of irrational fears. The fact that the patient could be influenced showed that a real attachment was present. This example is reminiscent of a mother calming her frightened child. Although the patient had made a relationship with the occupational therapist it was extremely vulnerable to the slightest stress. It was complicated by the fact that he sometimes confused her with some other real or imaginary figure. The tie was broken shortly after a weekend at home had to be cancelled. The patient felt the occupational therapist should have persuaded the writer to change his mind about this. The patient retired to bed and refused to get up. He was unwilling to see the occupational therapist when she came to visit him in the ward. The relationship was now ended.

Patients suffering from schizophrenia have not entirely given up attachments to others, as this example illustrates. However, the attachment is always weak and fragile. It may be broken at any moment. This is most often the result of anger following a disappointment. With patients who have been ill for a long time it may take months of constant attention from a psychiatrist or nurse before the patient is prepared to show the slightest interest. This contact which has been built up so slowly may be lost in a matter of seconds, the patient becoming completely inaccessible once again.

The barrier which obstructs communication between patient and psychiatrist or nurse may take other forms. In some cases the patient will speak but the form of his speech will be of such a nature as to preclude comprehension of its content. It may take a very long time before the psychiatrist comes to understand the patient's language and even then this understanding will only be partial. A further difficulty in the way of free communication is due to the patient casting the psychiatrist in the role of an enemy. The fact that the psychiatrist is responsible for the patient being confined to thc hospital provides a basis in reality for this belief.

Fortunately someone in the hospital usually does establish a relationship with the patient. It may be the ward maid or assistant nurse as frequently as the psychiatrist. Once a relationship has been established, the patient may begin to describe his experiences and provide an insight into the emotional problems connected with his symptoms. Occasionally the psychiatrist becomes the recipient of these confidences but, even when he is not, they need not be lost if the approach to the patient's treatment is based on close cooperation between nurses, doctors and supporting staff.

When he speaks, the patient demonstrates in the clearest possible manner that a change has affected his perception of himself *vis-à-vis* the outside world. He now feels himself to be the centre of events for reasons which he fails to understand. Other individuals and circumstances only enter into his thinking secondarily to an idea, perception, feeling or sensation about himself. His concern about others has been submerged by a preoccupation with himself. This preoccupation may consist of anxieties about his bodily integrity, his physical, sexual and personal identity, about his sexual feelings or about the effect of his anger on others.

These kinds of anxieties may arise in individuals who are not thought of as being schizophrenic. The schizophrenic patient is different in that he attributes these frightening changes to forces outside himself.

He believes that unknown or known agencies are trying to or have succeeded in altering his body, changing his identity, forcing him to accept unwelcome urges and ideas as his own, turning him into a woman, insinuating he is a homosexual or making him experience heterosexual or homosexual feelings against his will. He is convinced that his thoughts and actions can influence others, usually to their detriment.

In the following example it was possible to witness the concurrent expression of symptoms and certain preoccupations which were distressing to the patient. He was a single man of 23 years of age. He was brought to hospital because he had become increasingly withdrawn and strange in his behaviour. He was inclined to assume and maintain unusual postures for long periods of time. Later he explained he was practising Yoga exercises. I saw the patient frequently. The patient made no response; he was generally silent. Later, when he began to speak he might start a sentence and then stop in the middle without completing it. In the same way he halted movements half-way to completion. Eventually he said that I reminded him of a schoolmaster he disliked. This indicated his distaste for the meetings. Mostly he sat with his head bowed gazing vacantly out of the window. From the time of his admission this patient had shown much concern about his right hand and arm. He would inspect it closely, often holding it with his left hand as if it were paralysed. At other times the right arm was held rigidly flexed at the elbow. One day he expressed some of his fears in the following way: "I'm a homosexual, I'm frightened of real sex . . . it's all too much, I'm afraid of masturbating . . . I'll go mad, I've got to control myself." Later that day he smashed a window and then fell into a state of immobility.

As well as being concerned about the effect of their instinctual drives on themselves and on others, patients with schizophrenia frequently describe ideas about their parents which cause them (the patients) great distress. These fantasies assume all forms. Sometimes there is the thought that some change has affected one or other parent. The patient may believe that his father is a criminal, even a murderer, who has managed successfully to conceal his crimes. The father is consequently feared. He may be accused of being envious and jealous of the patient's good looks, youth and talents. Fears about the mother may take a different form. One patient had the fear that he might bite his mother, another that he would assault her sexually. A third patient thought his mother was subtly provoking him to attack her or to kill himself. In another instance the patient refused to believe that his father was dead. He was certain he had seen him in the street. When he did acknowledge his death he believed, like Hamlet, that his mother was in league with a man who had murdered his father. He attributed his symptoms to the fact that his mother, aware of his suspicions, was trying to kill him also.

Finally, reference should be made to those patients who claim that their parents are not their real parents. They insist that in infancy or childhood they were removed from their real parents and given to those who now claim them as children.

The patient not uncommonly experiences intense urges, sexual and aggressive, towards the parents, frequently towards the parent of the same sex. A young woman of 19 years of age who lived alone with her father, her mother having died a short time before, became very afraid of him. At first she feared that he might assault her sexually. She wondered if she were a homosexual and if everyone knew this and spoke about it. She heard people comment on her appearance and behaviour when she was out in the street. Finally she began to have sexual feelings towards her father.

The onset of a schizophrenic illness in adolescence or early adult life may be gradual or sudden. If it is gradual, the patient's personality appears to alter imperceptibly until he is quite detached from others, indifferent to his surroundings and without any desire to work or pursue formerly enjoyed interests. In such cases it is not always easy to discern the immediate causes for the illness. When the onset is sudden the occasion for the appearance of symptoms may be bereavement or a disappointment in love, pregnancy and childbirth, or serious illness in someone close to the patient. In those cases with no obvious precipitant it is only when the patient is able to express himself freely that the influences leading to the development of the illness become apparent. More often it appears that the patient is unable to overcome the challenges of adult life. He cannot reconcile himself to the demands of the sexual drives, the more so if they have a deviant expression. Competitiveness in society and arousal of aggression are other stresses which patients cannot tolerate. Why some individuals react to these stresses by developing a schizophrenic illness rather than a neurosis or behaviour disorder is entirely unknown.

The psychoanalytic interpretation

All the evidence suggests that schizophrenic illnesses have an immediate cause. In common with other theories of mental illness psychoanalysis distinguishes between the immediate cause and the predisposition to the illness. The predisposition is laid down in early life and is compounded of hereditary and environmental influences. It is always difficult to identify the predisposing causes with certainty as they arose in the distant past. It is easier to discern the exciting causes when the patient is able to relate his subjective experiences and information is available about his current life situation.

When the clinical phenomena are scrutinized it becomes apparent that patients suffering from schizophrenia are caught up in severe mental conflicts. These conflicts are not at the forefront of the patient's mind. He does not reflect on the idea that he is caught between a wish to carry out an act or obtain some form of pleasure on the one hand and a fear of the consequences or guilt on the other. He is only conscious of fear and guilt. He is aware of certain bodily sensations, urges, thoughts and feelings which are disturbing. He may acknowledge the origins within himself but insist that they were put there against his will by unknown forces. He may believe that he is being watched and threatened. He may hear voices criticizing him unjustly. When the circumstances of the patient's life immediately before the onset of the symptoms are known, they provide supporting evidence for the view that he has been in mental conflict. The kind of situation which is encountered has already been described. In every case the conflict involves other persons who are emotionally significant to the patient. The psychoanalytic view is that symptoms only make their appearance when certain intrapsychic conditions are established quite outside the patient's awareness. The sequence of events leading to an attack of schizophrenia may be best illustrated by taking as a clinical example a case where the immediate cause could be identified as a mental conflict which was beyond the patient's capacity to resolve.

The patient was a single woman of 24 years of age, a nursing sister by profession. Her father was a widower who lived alone but was looked after by a housekeeper. The patient came home every weekend. She had an attack of depression which necessitated hospital treatment. The exciting factor was the discovery that her father was having an affair with the housekeeper. After her discharge from hospital she became elated in mood and excited. She made a sexual advance to her father and then became profoundly depressed. When she returned to hospital she was seen regularly by a psychiatrist for some months until, unfortunately, he left the hospital and the meetings ceased. To this point there was no sign of serious mental derangement.

In the following weeks the patient accused the psychiatrist of inducing sexual arousal against her will, of making her pregnant and infecting her with venereal disease which led to an abortion. She was full of hate for the psychiatrist and insisted that even though he had left he was still able to influence her mind against her will. A few months later these ideas were transferred to the medical superintendent of the hospital who she said looked like her father. She said that the superintendent, a man in his middle sixties, was causing her to have homosexual sensations and was turning her into a prostitute. She complained of distressing bodily sensations which she attributed to the act of sexual intercourse proceeding between the superintendent and the matron of the hospital. It was of interest that about this time she spontaneously recalled witnessing her parents having sexual intercourse. The final development was her insistence that she was of royal parentage—her parents not being her real parents. She was aggressive in manner and difficult to make contact with.

The psychoanalytic interpretation places its main emphasis on two events in the patient's recent history. First, the discovery of the affair between father and housekeeper and, second, the relationship between patient and psychiatrist, both being closely interconnected. According to the psychoanalytic view, knowledge of her father's sexual life awakened memories of witnessing her parents' sexual intercourse. Memories of this event and the patient's horrified reaction to it were reported during her psychotic period. These memories were causally related to her delusion about the superintendent and the matron. The result of finding out about her father activated sexual and aggressive drives which, in turn, brought to life fantasies with a sadistic content. Though remaining unconscious they provoked the attack of depression. The meetings with the psychiatrist facilitated an arousal of those erotic and sadistic fantasies which, arising from the father in the first instance, were later to find another object in the person of the medical superintendent. The stage was set for the outbreak of symptoms before the departure of the psychiatrist. His leaving was regarded as a desertion in the same way as was the father's attachment to his housekeeper. The new disappointment evoked a fresh outburst of hatred which, in contrast to the earlier situation (discovering her father's affair with the housekeeper) could not be contained solely by the production of depressive symptoms. This time the hatred turned the loved object (the psychiatrist) into a persecutor and simultaneously resulted in an alienation from reality.

The psychoanalytic theory of psychosis postulates that it is the intensity of the sexual and aggressive drives which sets in motion the mechanisms which lead to symptom formation. The great strength of the drives creates a danger situation, the impact of which is no different from that which would arise from a real threat to bodily integrity. The drives are dangerous because early experience has given them this particular significance. In the mentally healthy and in those destined to develop neuroses, similar danger situations arise but are dealt with by repression—an automatic process whereby any traces of the feared ideas are removed from consciousness.

In psychosis, repression fails to prevent the entry of unwanted sensations, emotions and ideas into consciousness. The patient dreads the effect of his impulses on himself and others. In the absence of any effective means of countering the danger situation a movement takes place within the mind which initiates a breaking-down of all ties with those about him. The process continues until others, and the representation of those others within the mind, are deprived of all interest and emotional significance. Once this has occurred the environment and those in it are no longer assessed in terms of reality. From this point several different developments are possible. In the present case the withdrawal allowed the emergence of a mechanism whose effect was to help the patient believe that the dangerous impulses arose not from within herself but were directed into her from another source. The patient became the recipient rather than the originator of the unwanted mental contents. The danger was now experienced as coming from outside and the patient could disown all responsibility.

In other cases the withdrawal and disintegration of object ties lead to the employment of another means of dispelling the feared ideas from consciousness. In the case of the young woman who believed that she was a homosexual the danger situation was created by heterosexual impulses stimulated by proximity to her father. The incestuous wishes disappeared when she was preoccupied with the topic of homosexuality. She was able to achieve this relief by wholly identifying herself with her father. Once this happened she was only interested in women. Identification with the loved or lost individual is a common mechanism in psychotic illness. In schizophrenia it accounts for much of the frequency of preoccupation with homosexuality.

The change which affects the patient's attachment and concern for others is only one expression of the mental upheaval which occurs in schizophrenia. This 'internal catastrophe' as Freud[5] called it has other consequences. The self substitutes for others and becomes the focus of both love and hate. The resulting egocentrism influences thinking, speech, perception, memory and judgment. Thinking is no longer employed as trial action and speech is not regarded primarily as a means of communication. The similarities of these abnormal forms of cognition to the forms of cognition found in childhood have frequently been commented on by those who study schizophrenia. With interest and attention withdrawn from the environment, thinking becomes entirely the means of expressing wishes and fears. Thoughts have a greater significance for the patient than the facts of reality or the means (concepts) used to represent that reality in the mind. Behaviour is determined by this psychic reality and this leads to problems of adjustment. The patient's behaviour appears incomprehensible to others.

The clinical examples illustrate that alongside the disruption of ties with others a new psychotic or delusional reality develops. This psychotic reality, populated by real and imaginary figures both friendly and persecutory and in which the patient plays different roles, becomes a substitute for the lost attachments to real people. Many of the irrational ideas can be traced back to day-dreams the patient entertained years before the outbreak of the illness. Other features of the psychotic reality are derived from real experiences of childhood. The two processes of withdrawal and restitution, as they are called, do not take up all

61

the patient's mental life. My earlier examples showed that patients always retain a slender contact with others and this represents the remaining healthy mental life in them.

Psychoanalytic psychotherapy and management

It is essential to discover the strength of the remaining healthy life in the patient. The outcome of treatment will be entirely dependent on this factor. Recognition of conflicts and the means used to deal with them provides an understanding of the symptoms.

The treatment strategy for schizophrenics differs from that used for neurotics. In neurotic states the aim of psychoanalytic therapy is to make the patient aware of the connexions which exist between unconscious conflicts and the symptoms. This is achieved through the patient's recognition of his illness, and his wish to recover. A therapeutic alliance is formed between patient and therapist and it is this which allows the patient to examine his thoughts and feelings and give consideration to the analyst's interventions. Difficult times are tolerated during the treatment because of the bond which has been created between patient and analyst.

The situation is very different in cases of schizophrenia. The patient only rarely acknowledges that he is ill. The withdrawal and self-preoccupation means that for most of the time he is disinterested and no viable relationship develops between himself and the psychoanalyst. If an attachment occurs then treatment becomes a possibility. Examples have already been given where the patient made an attachment to a psychiatrist and to an occupational therapist. In such instances the treatment must be pursued within that relationship. The aim of the treatment is to strengthen the healthy aspects of the patient's mind through cultivating a relationship with him. This in itself deprives the dangerous fantasies of their strength and intensity. It is hoped that with the recovery of his grasp on reality, initially assisted by his bond with the therapist (whoever this is), the patient will come to re-evaluate and ultimately reject the delusional ideas.

The psychoanalytic treatment of schizophrenia is difficult and time-consuming with no guarantee of its even having a possible beginning quite apart from a favourable conclusion. In the United Kingdom, where mental hospitals are crowded and medical and nursing staff few, such treatments are virtually impossible. Treatment is confined to drugs or electroconvulsive therapy, which help the patient by reducing fear and dread but do not influence the ultimate outcome of the illness. Even under present conditions in mental hospitals, however, psychoanalysis has a vital part to play in the management of schizophrenic patients, through emphasizing the importance of cultivating their capacity to make attachments and through being aware of the dangers of aggravating the conflicts which disturb the patient. The psychoanalytic approach stresses the individuality of the patient and is critical of treatment regimes or discharge policies which are indiscriminately applied to all patients. Above all it provides guidelines which everyone—doctors, nurses, occupational therapists and all ward staff—can use in their dealings with the patient.

REFERENCES

1. BATCHELOR, I. R. C. (1964). *Proc. R. Soc. Med.* **57**, 147.
2. BLEULER, M. (1963). *Proc. R. Soc. Med.* **56**, 945.
3. FREUD, S. (1891). *On Aphasia: a Critical Study*. [1953. Authorized trans. Stengel, E. London: Imago].
4. FREUD, S. (1895). In *The Origins of Psycho-analysis*, ed. Bonaparte, M., Freud, A. and Kris, E. [1954. Authorized trans. Kris, E., pp. 349–445. London: Imago].
5. FREUD, S. (1911). In *Psychoanalytical Notes upon an Autobiographical Account of a Case of Paranoia*. [1958. In *Standard Edition*, vol. 12, pp. 3–82, ed. Strachey, J. and Freud, A. London: Hogarth.]

GENERAL REFERENCES

FREEMAN, T. (1969). *Psychopathology of the Psychoses*. London: Tavistock.

FREEMAN, T., CAMERON, J. L. and McGHIE, A. (1958). *Chronic Schizophrenia*. London: Tavistock.

8: Can Drugs Affect Personality?

C. R. B. JOYCE

THE short introductory paper that I contributed to one of our early meetings, to which visiting experts on various aspects of drug dependence were invited, was intended to establish a taxonomy of the drugs that are usually discussed under the heading 'drug dependence' but it had little to do with the basic problems confronting this working party. So a definite contribution to the book must now take a very different form, either 'hard', as scientific and objective as possible, or 'soft', subjective and polemical.

The presence of the concepts 'science' and 'personality' in our title (the latter, after all, has been given scientific definition—several of them[4]—by psychologists) ought to incline me without doubt to the former choice. The presence of scientists and representatives of non-scientific disciplines in our working party testifies to the intention to establish some kind of communication between the two. Yet though the attempts of most scientists to speak to their (in this sense) lay brothers are seldom impressive, it is even harder for the latter to adopt a scientific tradition and vocabulary in which they have not been trained in order to talk to scientists. But I am not convinced that the scientific language is appropriate to these discussions.

This is not a matter of condescension, but of conviction: of substance, not of style. Too often, it seems to me, in all the areas that matter to man, the requirements of the scientist that terms be defined with minute accuracy only lead to conclusions, if the experiment is performable at all, of outstanding triviality. On the other hand, although the relaxed and flowing statements of the humanists may be more stimulating, they seldom lead to hypotheses that are testable at all; and in the rare exception then only by personal experience, either of the individual or of society, and in such a way that the conclusions cannot be generalized and be shared with others or even found useful a second time by the same individual.

This book is one of many attempts to stitch the ancient wound. The division is particularly relevant to the relationship of drugs to personality, for 'experiments' with drugs are being carried out for the most part these days in a setting that is anything but 'experimental' in the scientific sense. I am not thinking here only of the millions of self-administrations of drugs made in non-medical situations and for non-medical reasons by all those who, in increasing numbers, are coming

65

to treat such experiences as part of their growing-up or of their post-adolescent daily life. Probably more than half the drugs that go down all the throats of the world every day are bought without prescription from chemists or other retailers by sick or healthy people who intend to medicate themselves. Each such episode is an experiment, just as for the illicit heroin or LSD user there is a hypothesis—that he will benefit, usually in some implicit way—a test and an outcome. But $n = 1$ in most cases, there are no controls and no exact replication; therefore, no valid scientific information results from such experiments.

Illicit drug use disturbs some people more than it disturbs others; scientists, as scientists, should be disturbed because it is not scientific. They should be similarly disturbed about legal self-medication of all kinds (of antibiotics as well as of psychotropics or drugs with reputed actions on the psyche) as well as about a great deal of medically prescribed and supervised drug-taking. It seems to me now highly significant that, just as most discussions of drug dependency confine themselves (whether accidentally or because in a self-perpetuating way more is known about that sub-area) to opiates, our own discussion of drugs and personality, though avoiding or at least aware of that trap, was still concerned only with drugs of dependence—even though mention was made of dependence on placebos.[6] The far more interesting problems about the deliberate use of drugs to change behaviour in a controlled way received practically no attention. I would like to redress the balance now.

In the most general terms, the questions that arise in regard to the use of drugs to change behaviour are those that also arise in connexion with the effects of surgery, of hormones, of education and other procedures used for the same purpose. They are: (a) When is it legitimate to use deliberate external means to modify behaviour? (b) When is it desirable to do this? (c) What means exist for the purpose? (d) Which, if any, will be effective?

Discussions of the first two of these questions form the subject matter of a great part of this book. In principle (which is far from saying in practice) I take the view that it is legitimate and indeed compulsory to modify an individual's behaviour if the argument of numbers is compelling (that is, if two people will be saved by the change, even if it means the perdition of one other) and especially if the procedure proposed is reversible or if its unwanted effects can be handled in an acceptable way should they occur. In other words, my answer to the first question reduces to the second. I shall say no more about either here but confine myself to the fourth, and to the third in so far as drugs are concerned.

Can drugs be used to change personality? I was careful, in the previous paragraph, to refer to changes in behaviour rather than in personality. There is no point, nor any need, to involve ourselves in linguistic discussions, but I had two reasons for making the distinction. I do not think personality should be changed, nor do I think it can be, at least not in any desirable direction. This is an important qualification.

A relevant definition of personality is necessary; here is one. Personality is an abstraction from an individual's total set of attributes, physical and psychological, that enable that individual or an outside observer to predict with better than chance success what his reactions will be to any specified circumstances.

This definition means that the individual's response to drugs, in so far as it is predictable, is itself a manifestation of his personality. The individual with a personality that includes the trait technically defined as extraversion[3] responds to a small amount of alcohol with aggression or other forms of disinhibition, while the individual whose personality includes the approximately contrary trait, introversion, can take alcohol, or others of the so-called 'depressant' drugs, without becoming less gentlemanly as the evening goes on.

But this definition has not been carefully chosen so that it can be used just at a merely semantic level, to show that the proposition about drugs is true. There would be no point in such a definition. Its triviality is shown by considering the case in which a new drug that possesses a totally original kind of action is used—something which does occur from time to time although not very frequently. It would be most unsatisfactory to claim in such circumstances that the drug has no effect on personality simply because its mode of action is so new that there is no information on which to predict the change in the individual's behaviour that it may cause.

An argument of somewhat more value, on the other hand, would begin by emphasizing the ability, justified by much experimental evidence, of many drugs to increase the variability of behaviour and in so doing to reduce its predictability. Such an increase in variability of behaviour is often desirable, but even the claims of those who promote variability and new sensations at all costs are somewhat limited by the difficulty of demonstrating, as in the case of genetic mutations, that variability is of value to an individual, or to the society of which he or she is a member, if altered behaviour of potential value cannot be selected. In the latter case this is ensured, according to classical ideas, by the processes of natural selection and in the former by what the psychologist refers to as reinforcement: in other words, by the reliable association of some value-conferring contingency, via the behaviour, with the stimulus that has elicited it. The particularly relevant instance, in discussing the effect of drugs on personality, is so-called state-dependent learning.[5] There seems to be evidence that learning that occurs in a 'drugged' state does not transfer, or does not fully transfer, to situations in which the drug is absent. This, if true, has profound consequences for the use of drugs to modify behaviour in a social or clinical setting. It is not yet, however, clear whether learning of any kind is state-dependent.[9] Even if such a phenomenon does occur, it is still not clear whether the failure to show a transfer of learning from the occasions where drugs are present to those from which they are absent is due to the non-occurrence of stimuli associated with the presence of the drug, with the occurrence of new factors in the environment which were not present with the drug, or are related to the drug in a secondary fashion.

The logical consequences seem to be as follows: (a) if state-dependent learning does not occur at all, there are no situations in which the use of drugs can confer benefits which cannot be obtained in other ways; (b) if it does occur, but is due to the absence of certain non-drug factors from or the presence of new ones in the non-drug state, the said non-drug factors are operating in a direction opposite to that of the drug itself. Their successful identification and introduction into the non-drug situation should then facilitate the previously learned behaviour, and it should therefore have been possible to bring about this facilitation without the use of drugs in the first place; and (c) if state-dependent learning does occur, and if the difference between the two states is directly due to the presence or absence of the drug itself, then the drugs initially used cannot subsequently be withdrawn if the behaviour that has been changed is still to persist.

We live in a society that uses drugs on an enormous scale. The implications of this for physical psychiatry and for philosophy may need to be carefully considered. But it would not necessarily be a bad society that permitted the continued use of a given drug from cradle, or at least from first necessity, to grave. This is, in any event, what happens to those patients who must take hormone supplements or replacements because their own secretion is inadequate, or who receive a drug supplement the action of which differs only in degree from these, for example a diuretic or a cardiotonic agent. Millions of patients also receive major tranquillizers continuously for major affective disorders.

We therefore need to inquire (a) whether the reasons for which these drugs are being given are justified; and (b) whether the changes in patients' behaviour that they produce are in a desirable or undesirable direction. A great many prescriptions are probably written for chronic schizophrenics because they make such people less of a threat to society or because they enable society itself to contain them. This comes about because the variability of their behaviour is in fact actually being reduced. In the process they may or may not become happier but, even if they do, an increase in happiness does not necessarily indicate a desirable change in personality. Happiness is a response to a change in state—it contains no information about the nature of the change as such.

With some exceptions, too, whether the modified behaviour that such drugs produce represents an increase or a reduction in variability, it is seldom followed by any attempt to select those aspects which are individually or socially desirable in any planned form. (We are of course still concerned with the possibility rather than the propriety of such actions.) A recent book[7] emphasizes the view that psychotherapy may often be a necessary introduction to pharmacotherapy, just as pharmacotherapy may pave the way for subsequent psychotherapy. One may have to talk patients into receiving drugs or one may have to use drugs in order to persuade them to listen at all. My present case is that if drugs are used to pave the way for 'talk', it is the talk that eventually produces the change in personality; and that if talk precedes the pharmacology, pharmacology itself will lead to nothing unless it is succeeded by another period of talk. Even in the clinically rare event that this occurs,[1] the second situation reduces to the first.

To me it seems no more surprising that drugs should be inadequate for the purpose of changing personality than that some of the other methods (leucotomy, castration and so on) discussed in this volume should prove so too. All these methods are, after all, exceedingly gross: however excellent the original intentions, quite apart from the diversity or specificity of the results, the consequences of cutting a nervous tract, of removing the testes, or of administering a substance the action of which is distributed throughout the body and as a rule very widely through the whole brainstem itself, cannot induce changes of behaviour which are under fine and sensitive adjustment. The ears and eyes lead directly to the central nervous system and to very specific areas within that system; the veins, the rectum and the mouth do not. Fortunately the ears and eyes have other materials poured into them more frequently than drugs.

It is by no means impossible that with increasing knowledge we shall be able to achieve a much finer degree of adjustment of behaviour by the use of locally applied drugs, for which the exciting techniques of Bradley[2] and of Olds[8] and their followers have already begun to pave the way. But even to approximate the fine adjustments that are already possible with words, it will be necessary to apply microdoses of nucleic acids or other chemicals, not merely intracellularly, and not merely to one or to ten specific cells, but to hundreds or thousands of cells whose location and functions have been precisely identified and the time relations between the activity and refractoriness of which have also been fully analysed. The sequences of drug administration will therefore have to to carried out with exquisite accuracy, no doubt under the control of computer monitoring systems. Meanwhile, words and gestures are the most delicate instruments we have and are likely to remain so for a long time.

It may appear strange for a pharmacologist to speak in this way.

To those who resolutely continue to 'experiment' (in the way defined at the outset) with centrally active drugs of their own or of another's choice, it may seem especially strange. After all, the knowledge they have themselves acquired tells them that certain drugs reliably make available sights and sounds and other experiences to which they would otherwise never have access. But these experiences cannot be externalized. However valid they are for the individual in whom they occur they cannot be communicated to the outside world. Most of us are familiar with attempts to do this. The distinguishing features of paintings and drawings produced by even the most talented artists while under the influence of LSD, for example, include either a clear loss of basic skills, a reduction of complexity (otherwise put—a loss of information) or a set of statements which are fragmentary, disconnected and very difficult to understand using the rules of syntax and interpretation which apply in normal circumstances. That they have little validity even for others in a similar state, or for the individual himself on another occasion, is witnessed by the frequent inability of either to interpret such statements at other times.

I conclude by deliberately breaching the shaky wall of my own arguments. Up to the present I have largely been restricting the discussion of personality to cognitive terms, and this may be offensive—perhaps rightly so—to those who hold that one should at least admit the participation of the emotions in personality, if not their primacy. A possible relationship between some of the many factors involved may be represented as in Fig. 1. Level 1 represents a genetic component, which provides a relatively constant physiological and biochemical basis. Level 2 is a rapidly oscillating measure which may describe, in technical as well as in common speech, emotional changes. The periodicity of these fluctuations may be measured in seconds, or perhaps in minutes at most. At level 3, a function with a longer frequency of variation describes changes in what can similarly be called mood. Between this and level 6, the function describing personality-state itself, there is a whole range of other events having a longer and longer periodicity; these can be typified by levels 4 and 5, for which, interestingly, no convenient figures of speech seem to exist. Personality (level 6) is represented by a curve with a single inflexion (one might perhaps allow it two). Level 7 represents the sum of all these: it may be referred to as the curve of behaviour. Like any other curve, it can be submitted to frequency analysis, and the components which will then be extracted from it depend upon the assumptions on which the analysis is based. In this case, since a curve has been constructed that sums all those below it, to extract frequency components from the sum will tell us nothing further. But although the information content remains a matter of belief, two factors in particular determine the general shape

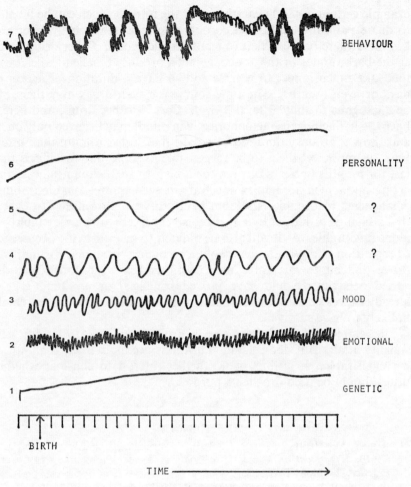

FIG. 1. For explanation see text.

and position of curve 7. Curve 1, the genetic background, sets the baseline upon which the other curves oscillate; curve 6, here called personality, sets the general trend. It should be added that some would hold level 6 itself to be the sum of all those below it, and the same could be said of levels 5, 4, and so on, in turn. But the main point, which is seen as soon as we consider the many other factors that act and interact with those listed above, is unaffected by this argument. The food the individual eats will interact with his biochemistry and modify it, as will the drugs he takes. His life states, from moment to moment or from year to year, will modify by their stress and ease of stress the picture of his behaviour. The fluctuations that they produce will also have a characteristic periodicity. The duration of action of some drugs, for

71

example certain general anaesthetics or the nitrites which can be inhaled to dilate painfully contracted coronary vessels, is extremely brief and lies somewhere between that of emotion and mood. Other drugs, such as the barbiturates or the anticoagulants, produce biochemical changes that take much longer to reverse and so have a duration of action of days or even months. The time-course for such drugs may therefore be analogous to that of level 3 or 4. Certain other drugs, and here I have the hallucinogens metaphorically in mind, may be given only once, and show a primary duration of action that lasts no more than a few hours at most, yet seem to be responsible in some way for effects that last for months or years or even for life.[10] In such circumstances, and acting upon such a complex substrate, it seems unreasonable (though what seems reasonable is seldom likely to be reason itself) to expect that a change produced by any drug is very likely to be predictable, let alone favourable. As it will also be difficult to guarantee the occurrence or repetition of any such changes in a recognizably similar form, it will prove difficult to guarantee their reinforcement. Thus, whether the varied behaviour would have proved beneficial or not (and I have already expressed the personal opinion that it would not), it is extremely unlikely to have survived.

The simple and unqualified use of drugs is unlikely to modify personality at all. If it does, the modifications are more likely than not to be undesirable. It is thus of no further interest to consider whether drugs should be used for such a purpose.

REFERENCES

1. BALINT, M., HUNT, J., JOYCE, C. R. B., MARINKER, M. and WOODCOCK, J. J. (1970). *Treatment or Diagnosis: a Study of Repeat Prescriptions in General Practice.* London: Tavistock.

2. BRADLEY, P. B. and WOLSTENCROFT, J. H. (1965). *Br. med. Bull.* **21**, 15.

3. EYSENCK, H. J. (1957). *The Dimensions of Anxiety and Hysteria.* London: Routledge.

4. FOSS, B. M. (1968). In *Psychopharmacology: Dimensions and Perspectives*, chap. 2. ed. Joyce, C. R. B. London: Tavistock.

5. GIRDEN, E. and CULLER, E. A. (1937). *J. comp. Psychol.* **23**, 261.

6. JOYCE, C. R. B. (1969). In *Scientific Basis of Drug Dependence*, pp. 271–279, ed. Steinberg, H. London: Churchill.

7. KLEIN, D. F. and DAVIS, J. M. (1969). *Diagnosis and Drug Treatment of Psychiatric Disorders.* Baltimore: Williams and Wilkins.

8. OLDS, J. (1959). *Neuropsychopharmacology* **1**, 2032.

9. OVERTON, D. A. (1968). In *Psychopharmacology: a Review of Progress 1957–1967*, pp. 918–930, ed. Efron, D. H. Washington, D.C.: Public Health Service Publication No. 1836.

10. SNYDER, S. (1970). In *Hallucinogenic Drug Research*, p. 13, eds Gamage, J. R. and Zerkin, E. L. Beloit: Stash Press.

9: Drugs of Addiction: General Discussion

THE working party discussed various aspects of this subject, with guest speakers, over several sessions. Some of these discussions are summarized in this chapter.

The old definitions of drugs of addiction (drugs whose withdrawal induces physical symptoms which are roughly the reverse of the effects of the drug) and non-addictable drugs (whose withdrawal does not induce bodily symptoms) are no longer adequate. Physiological and psychological dependence, though slightly more appropriate terms, grossly oversimplify the complex condition of drug dependence. Psychological and physical effects of some drugs merge in varying proportions in different individuals and even in the same individual at different times.

HARD-DRUG ADDICTION

The mechanisms by means of which subjects with mental illness recover are mostly unknown, and this is certainly true for recovery from drug addiction. One of the factors that seems to be associated with recovery in hard-drug users is a stable premorbid personality (as in subjects in whom addiction is established through medical prescription of a drug). Other important factors may include compulsory but caring supervision, within the community, by a trained individual (for example, a probation officer); continuous employment within the community; the development of a close, stable relationship with someone, for example a wife or colleague, in the community or with a group substituted for the drug-taking group. The latter may be a self-contained religious body, such as a small, rigid sect of a nonconformist Church. It is unusual for cured addicts to feel that they have derived any help from close relatives such as their parents, or from psychiatrists or other doctors.

DRUGS AND THE COMMUNITY

The community's attitude to drug taking is ambivalent, with the result that, in practice, it is neither reasonable nor consistent. The community tends to regard all drugs of dependence and all situations in which they are taken as presenting similar problems, and this increases the confusion. Polydrug experimentation in young people, for example, is a different problem from long-term drug dependence. Young people experiment with drugs but most of them give this up as they grow older and more mature. If we accept the individual's right to experiment, then we must accept drug taking and the continual presence of some addicts in the community. A plateau level for drug taking is therefore inevitable in a free society but we should aim to keep the level as low as possible. This also means that, however successful our research into the causation of drug taking, we may have to accept the permanent need for treatment centres.

The number of people in a given community who regularly take drugs affecting the central nervous system will depend on certain characteristics peculiar to that community at that particular time. For example, drug taking will be related to such factors as the amount of deviant behaviour acceptable to a community and the alternative activities it provides. In many Western countries the ingestion of alcohol as well as cigarette smoking (alternative activities) are currently fairly acceptable, and drug taking is regarded as degrading; whereas in Moslem countries hashish smoking is readily accepted and the drinking of alcohol is not.

There are highly complex and overlapping reasons for the current cult of drug taking in young people in such countries as the United States and the United Kingdom. The stresses of overcrowding may increase the need for alternative activities (*v.s.*). Many young people take drugs in protest against society; or to express their need to belong to a particular group (that is, one which takes drugs). They may experiment with drugs hoping that this will increase their self-understanding, or they may be looking for an (idealized) escape from their problems. Increased self-understanding may occasionally be achieved with a drug like LSD but this is probably more because of the subject's positive expectations than the drug's pharmacological effects. Thus, drug addiction reflects various needs in the addict (for self-discovery, experimentation, human warmth, the need to belong to a group, or a search for identity). These needs are clearly not being adequately met by contemporary social institutions and structures. Research into and proposals for changes in society's role are needed. The law could perhaps enlarge its role as a framework within which social conscience can act. The law is society's protector and exists also to protect the freedom of the individual. It should not work as an organ of retribution but as a means for highlighting conditions in which society can show its concern.

Community treatment

A hopeful approach in the management of hard-drug addicts has been used at the Addiction Unit, All Saints' Hospital, Birmingham, England. Dr John Owens and his colleagues have set up a programme of community treatment in which psychiatrists at the Unit and various non-medical personnel in Birmingham have established a good and effective working relationship. Nurses, social workers, pharmacists, probation officers, the police, and many socially oriented groups, as well as the general public, have all worked together with the hospital-based team. This close cooperation between the police drug squad and the personnel of this Addiction Unit is impressive and unusual. The registered drug addicts, rather surprisingly, seemed to derive a sense of security from their knowledge of this cooperation. They knew that if they were charged with an offence they would get a fair chance to establish their innocence and, if guilty, receive appropriate treatment for their addiction. Every patient also knew that if he was in genuine difficulty at awkward places, or unusual times, he could always contact a member of the drug squad who would give honest and helpful assistance, even to the extent of bringing the patient to the clinic. The staff of the clinic work as a team and the patients knew and accepted that they would not necessarily be seen by the same person, medical or non-medical, every time they needed help. This acceptance that they would still get help even if their own particular doctor was not available also increased their sense of security. And this added security felt by the patients did much to dispel some of the fears of professional workers in this field. As a voluntary measure, Birmingham successfully restricted the prescribing of hard drugs to a small number of authorized doctors, and hard-drug dispensing to a few authorized pharmacists, several years before the practice was adopted by law in the rest of the United Kingdom.

LEGAL ASPECTS

Legal policy is based on *possession* of any amount of an illegal drug, not on misuse or overdose, as with alcohol. It might be more realistic to change the law so that it is illegal to have taken more than a specified amount of a given drug (as revealed by urine or blood tests) or to possess more than a specified, but of course larger, amount of the drug without having taken it (suggesting that the individual is selling rather than just using it). In the meantime, a more lenient enforcement of the law, especially for soft drugs such as cannabis, might be appropriate. In effect this would leave enforcement of the law largely to the discretion of the police or the Director of Public Prosecutions. The Director of Public Prosecutions and the police do already exercise some discretion in bringing criminal charges which, in practice, makes the administration of the criminal law workable. This procedure has to be recognized when discussing the self-evident fact that a non-enforced law undermines the legal system. There is a marked difference between the exercise of this discretion and non-enforcement of the law.

Although in practice blood and urine testing for drugs in suspected addicts would protect them from being falsely charged, blood testing without an individual's consent is, in English law, a criminal assault unless special legislative provisions have been made. If the subject is a minor, this consent can only be given by his parents or legal guardian.*

* See also p. 78.

10: Some Legal Observations on the Effects of Science on Personality

T. E. JAMES

It is well recognized that the law is not always at its best when it deals explicitly with large philosophical issues such as the freedom of the individual. The legal system is one method whereby individual or group activities are encouraged or discouraged. There is no doubt that the law tends to follow, rather than to act as an innovator of, ideological or economic developments. Legally, underlying the discussion on Personality and Science, the question repeatedly protrudes: what are the limits placed by the law upon the individual's freedom to act as best pleases him? The point has been made by an eminent lawyer that, if we wish to preserve the liberty of the subject in conditions of Western civilization today, some restrictions on that liberty are essential. Lord Radcliffe in his book *The Law and Its Compass*[17] observes: "If the liberal society is to continue to take its stand on tolerance, it is very necessary that its members should be continuously aware of what is involved in this strange and exacting conception." In this connexion a distinction must be drawn between tolerance and indifference.

In pursuing the question of the effect of science on personality, developments in knowledge and/or techniques were central to the discussions. The developments the working party selected were those considered to be imminent and most likely to invite philosophical and ethical considerations. Thus, preceding chapters have discussed temporal lobectomy and leucotomy, castration and sterilization, the effect of drugs, endocrine disorders and behaviour, and, as an example of psychosis, schizophrenia.

These topics raise serious problems for the law, and eminent lawyers, for example Lord Devlin and Professor Glanville Williams (a reference to the transactions of the Medico-Legal Society will supply many other names) have tried to crystallize the issues involved. It may be, as Lord Radcliffe has observed, that the principles of the law, which are no more than generalizations relating to human conduct, cannot sustain the weight of reasoning that is today brought to bear upon them. Statute has certainly intervened in no small way to supplement these general principles as, for example, by the Race Relations Act (1965), which may be regarded as both social and educative legislation. Perhaps the legislature has been particularly active in this respect in the field of criminal offences imposing strict or absolute liability, not requiring proof of knowledge or *mens rea*.

The attitude of the law today as regards drugs is an apt illustration. It may be summed up in the words of Lord Parker, Chief Justice: "I certainly take judicial notice of the fact that drugs are a great danger today, and legislation has been tightening up the control of drugs in all its aspects" (*Yeandel* v. *Fisher*[26]). This case involved a charge of being concerned in the management of premises (a public house) which were used for the purpose of smoking cannabis, contrary to what is now the Dangerous Drugs Act, 1965 (section 5). The interpretation of this section has given rise to concern, especially when it is used against private houses.

The lawyer finds the situation disquieting, but for other reasons. In *Yeandel* v. *Fisher*[26] the court held that "Legislation had in mind making those, at any rate who were on the spot and concerned with the management of premises, absolutely liable." That is, the offence is one of strict or absolute liability, not requiring proof of knowledge or *mens rea*. As Lord Parker put it, in deciding whether an offence "is in fact an absolute offence or whether *mens rea* in the true sense is involved . . . depends upon the words of the particular statute and the subject-matter with which it is dealing." Because drugs are a great danger and public welfare is concerned, protective prohibitions are to be presumed to impose strict liability.

This attitude was extended to the case of persons found in possession of prohibited drugs without being duly authorized (contrary to section 13 and the schedules to the Dangerous Drugs Act, 1965; and see *R.* v. *Warner*[25]). Some alleviation of the harsh results of this attitude has been provided by the House of Lords' decision in *R.* v. *Warner*. 'Possession' must be understood as of being knowingly in control of a thing in circumstances which have involved an opportunity (whether availed of or not) to learn or to discover, at least in a general way, what the thing is. It follows that if there is assent to the control of a thing, either having the means of discovering what the thing contains or being indifferent whether there are means of knowledge or not, then ordinarily there will be possession within the meaning of the statute. Thus, drugs *planted* on someone would not be in his possession. Apart from this, lack of knowledge only goes in mitigation of sentence.

Some limitation has been put by the courts upon this doctrine of possession; for example, a passenger in a car which, unknown to him, is carrying drugs is not sufficiently in control of them to be in possession (*R.* v. *Prevost*[23]). Again, to establish that a person who owns a room in a house is in possession of drugs found therein, he must be shown to have known he was in possession of the thing (for example, a parcel) which is proved to contain the dangerous drugs (*R.* v. *Smith*[24]).

A more liberal construction of 'in possession' by the courts or new legislation requiring some knowledge of the existence of drugs might allay anxieties on this score (see Misuse of Drugs Bill, 1970). The main reason for the present situation is that it is tolerably plain that there must be many statutory prohibitions which would be incapable of enforcement if the prosecution had to adduce evidence to prove facts which are peculiarly within the knowledge of the accused.

It is in furtherance of attempts to deal with the accepted danger of drugs today that the police are given power to stop and search without warrant any person suspected of being in unlawful possession of drugs, and that powers to enter and search certain premises are provided.[14]

A principle generally accepted by the law and jealously regarded is that what people choose to do to themselves in private is their own business, provided it is not criminal *per se* (*R. v. Donovan*,[22] *v. i.*) nor harmful to others. The fact that the conduct is criminal *per se* would be another concept than that it is harmful to society in general. This latter category would include, for example, a conspiracy to pervert public morals. It would be hard to see why the law should interfere if the activity in question were not causing trouble to anyone or to society in general, but the problem involved would be concerned with the concept of public welfare at any given time. In relation to drugs this can only be answered by the scientific knowledge and findings of those who specialize in this field. The thoughtful report on cannabis by the Hallucinogens Subcommittee (chairman, Lady Wootton) of the Advisory Committee on Drug Dependence[13] is really based on these considerations.

Since alcoholism and cigarette smoking are so frequently adduced as parallels to drug addiction, it is perhaps worthy of comment that the charge is often made that some sections of the medical profession have softened up the public to an increase of drug taking, thereby misleading the addict by the false notion that there is a pill or potion for the avoidance of every discomfort.[10] The use of opium in the nineteenth century is extremely well illustrated by Alethea Hayter in her excellent book.[12] The suspicion is raised that it is not only in our generation that the idea of the good society has never been completely free of external stimulants, whether these are produced from opium or other such drugs.

The legal questions raised by the operations discussed in this volume (castration, leucotomy and temporal lobectomy) which are irreversible, involve a consideration of ordinary (that is, generally accepted) and experimental operations. The effects of hormone administration, or drug treatment for schizophrenia, need not presumably be permanent. There are, further, the more subtle forms of treatment which result in changes of personality to some extent, for example dynamic psychotherapy and behaviour therapy. However, if this line of reasoning is pursued, the question of religious persuasion, considered in its therapeutic aspect, could also be included. It is not the function of the law to lay down the rules relating to the purpose of human existence, namely the individual's happiness; the law aims rather at allowing the individual the freedom of choice, protecting the freedom of every man to discern what is good and choose for himself within certain vague limits. It is the vagueness of the limits which poses the problem for the judge and the legislature. "For it is in the education of individual character, the slow persuasion of the public conscience, that this society has chosen to find its sustaining ideal."[17] The lawyer would surely regard himself as an important instrument in pursuing this aim.

Thus, in surgical or therapeutic treatment there is legal liability, which may be civil or criminal. The former is relatively straightforward: the action in tort would usually be for negligence or assault. A person who holds himself out as ready to give medical advice or treatment implies that he is possessed of skill and knowledge for the purpose. If a surgeon performs an operation without his patient's consent or implied consent, he is guilty of trespass. Consent is implied in the sense that a surgeon would be assumed "to do everything in his power to remove the mischief, provided that he had no absolute definite instructions not to operate" (*Beatty* v. *Cullingworth*).[2] The case was an action for damages by a nurse for assault and negligence by a surgeon who removed one ovary with express consent and then, finding the other infected, removed it. In these civil cases, therefore, the cause of action is removed by the patient's consent: *volenti non fit injuria*. Difficulties may arise when the patient has not the capacity to consent.

Liability in criminal law is complicated and unclear; moreover, it is made more uncertain by the changing attitude of the public, the legislature and the medical profession itself. This change is apparent, for example, in relation to legislation on abortion or in correspondence on sterilization in the *British Medical Journal* (see Editorial[11]).

It seems well established in English law that the consent of the person to an act, which is unlawful in the sense of being itself a criminal act, cannot render that act lawful (*R.* v. *Coney*;[20] *R.* v. *Donovan*[22]). In the eyes of the law anyone who touches the human body assaults or batters it and, *prima facie*, commits a wrongful act, which it is for him to justify. The usual justification of a surgical operation is the consent of the patient. It is the essence of assault and battery that they are done against the will of the victim (*Christopherson* v. *Bare*[6]). Further, it is a sufficient defence to a charge of assault that the act alleged was a mere accident or that it was done while the parties were engaged in a game or sport which was lawful and not seriously dangerous to life or limb. Thus, in *R.* v. *Coney*[20] it was held that all persons aiding and abetting prize-fighting, which was illegal, were guilty of assault and that the consent of the persons engaged in fighting did not afford a defence. This is an illustration of the fact that there may be some cases of assault which are *per se* unlawful, to which consent would be no defence. This aspect of the law was discussed in *R.* v. *Donovan*[22] where there was an alleged assault by the accused, who had caned a young girl with her consent. The Court of Criminal Appeal was not prepared to hold that the alleged assault could be regarded as *per se* criminal without evidence that the blows struck were likely or intended to do bodily harm to the girl. In this context, bodily harm has its ordinary meaning and includes any hurt or injury calculated to interfere with the health or comfort of the victim; such hurt need not be permanent but must be more than merely transient and trifling.

The problem as to what conduct is *per se* criminal is clouded by the concept of public policy. The surgeon has to consider whether such operations as leucotomy or castration are contrary to public policy and therefore *per se* criminal. There are well-established exceptions to the general rule that an act likely or intended to cause bodily harm is an unlawful act, for example the playing of games such as Rugby football or baseball, and the reasonable chastisement of a child by a parent or persons *in loco parentis* (*R.* v. *Donovan*[22]). Moreover, in an abortion case prior to the Abortion Act (1967), a prosecution was dismissed where the surgeon performed the operation, having reasonable grounds and adequate knowledge that the probable consequence of pregnancy would make the woman a physical or mental wreck (*R.* v. *Bourne*[19]).

It would seem that irreversible operations could be safely performed if they were for therapeutic purposes; but this would scarcely cover cases involving, for example, change-of-sex operations in England at the present time unless there were perhaps an overriding social necessity, as in the case of castration of the so-called sexual psychopath (see *R.* v. *Cowburn*[21]), sexual deviants and morons. However, this latter class of cases would have to be carefully watched to see that there was no kind of coercion.

There is no reported legal case involving castration, though the Court of Criminal Appeal has been asked to give its blessing to the performance in prison of such an operation, which might have had the effect of curing the accused and which he was prepared to undergo (*R.* v. *Cowburn*[21]). The court refused to accede to this request and observed that what took place in prison was not its concern. The accused in this case was apparently a psychopath with uncontrollable sexual impulses. The medical reports suggested that there were only two possible solutions in his case: hormone treatment or castration. He seemed to have been willing to undergo the latter. The need to obtain the court's approval arose from the uncertainty of the law on this point and the fears of the prison authorities that such an operation might be unlawful or contrary to public policy. It has been suggested, following an observation by Lord Justice Denning (now Lord Denning) in a divorce case involving sterilization, that "an ordinary surgical operation, which is done for

81

the sake of a man's health, with his consent, is, of course, perfectly lawful because there is just cause for it" (*Bravery* v. *Bravery*[4]).

It would seem most doubtful whether, in England today, the facts of *R*. v. *Cowburn*[21] could provide a just cause for the operation. It is true that the forcible feeding of a suffragette prisoner could be justified on the grounds that it was necessary to preserve the health of the prisoner in custody and, *a fortiori*, to preserve her life (*Leigh* v. *Gladstone*[15]). Further, it would appear that even if the measures taken were incidentally to shorten her life, a doctor is entitled to do all that is proper and necessary to relieve pain and suffering (*R*. v. *Adams*[18]). Castration has, however, been condemned by legal writers of the highest authority;[3, 8] but the grounds for the condemnation may have been public policy,[7] namely, depriving the king of a fighting man.

It is true that the law and practice appear to be modifying in relation to operations designed to sterilize the patient on eugenic grounds. Voluntary sterilization has never been declared by the English courts to be lawful nor has there been any legislation to authorize such operations, which are known to take place despite the recommendations of the report of the departmental committee on sterilization.[9] But the legality of a sterilization operation which is necessary for the patient's treatment (therapeutic sterilization) would seem to be established.[2, 9] A statement by the Secretary of the Medical Defence Union on behalf of its Council[1] gives some indication of the change in feeling towards eugenic sterilization. This type of operation is performed not necessarily for the patient's health but to prevent propagation of unsound offspring. The Council of the Medical Defence Union has advised that an operation for sterilization is lawful, whether it is performed on therapeutic or eugenic grounds, or for any other reason, provided there is full and valid consent to the operation by the patient. It is possible that castration may in the future be subject to a similar change of feeling.

However, in England at least, there is no statute which specifically controls the conditions under which experimental operations can be performed. Leucotomy is a case in point and has undoubtedly been accepted as a recognized form of treatment in certain cases. The criminal law has certainly not been invoked, despite the permanent effect of this operation, which still appears to be in an experimental stage.[16]

As regards castration, it is true that other countries have performed such operations and published some material. The work in Denmark is particularly well known. In these countries such operations are provided for, in proper circumstances, by statute. The results, however, do not seem to be sufficiently convincing as yet to the medical and, in consequence, to the legal profession in England. In this regard, the report from Norway[5] of a follow-up study which revealed a number of examples illustrating the wide margin of uncertainty existing in psychiatric diagnosis and prognosis should be mentioned. It is possible, should a specific category of case be defined in which castration might be of benefit, that some change in attitude in England respecting these operations will take place. In the present state of knowledge, treatment with drugs is generally considered more suitable than an operation of a permanently enduring nature. As Dr A. Hyatt Williams, an eminent British psychiatrist, observed (personal communication): "Castration is to stilboestrol (a hormone) what leucotomy is to Largactil (a tranquillizer)."

Apart from irreversible treatment, there is the problem of the therapeutic use of drugs. It would seem that the consent of the patient, together with the fact that reputable members of the medical profession approve the treatment as therapeutic, would be sufficient in the eyes of the law. As in psychoanalytic treatment, however, it is possible that some of the methods would so alter the personality that the treatment might be considered irreversible. Here, in relation to treatment, the subject of imprisonment would be in point. This perhaps raises certain aspects of behaviour therapy. Good evidence exists that a long sentence of imprisonment (five years or more) does in fact effect changes in the personality of the offender, whether for good or bad. It would be harder to say that other institutional treatments (in borstals, approved schools, detention centres) or, indeed, shorter terms of imprisonment have this effect. Many persons in the penological field, of course, assume that institutional treatment can have a beneficial effect in some cases. Here a clear distinction must be made between cases said to be institutionalized for their own treatment and those who are deprived of liberty because of the need to protect the public from their activities.

In conclusion, it seems that a distinction must be drawn between established and recognized therapeutic operations, and experimental operations. In the latter category leucotomy may be cited, and the problems involved may be well illustrated by the present much-discussed heart transplant operation. The law, as regards experimental operations, places a heavy burden of proof on the medical profession to show the therapeutic value of the procedure (for example, castration). The phrase medical profession would here include all those persons engaged in the study and treatment of mental and physical illness, including the psychiatrist and the psychoanalyst.

REFERENCES

1. ADDISON, P. H. (1966). *Br. med. J.* **2**, 1597.

2. BEATTY V. CULLINGWORTH (1896). *Br. med. J.* x, 1546.

3. BLACKSTONE, W. (1773). In *Commentaries on the Laws of England*, 5th edn, **4**, 206. Oxford: Clarendon Press.

4. BRAVERY V. BRAVERY [1954]. 1 W.L.R. 1169, 1180, C.A.

5. BREMER, J. (1959). *Asexualization*. New York: Macmillan.

6. CHRISTOPHERSON V. BARE [1848]. 11 Q.B. 473.

7. COKE, E. (1823). In *Institutes of the Laws of England* (18th edn, ed. Butler, C.), **1**, 127*a*, *b*. London: J. and W. T. Clarke; R. Theney; and S. Brooke.

8. COKE, E. (1823). In *Institutes of the Laws of England* (18th edn, ed. Butler, C.), **3**, 118. London: J. and W. T. Clarke; R. Theney; and S. Brooke.

9. Cmd 4485 (1933). *Report of the Departmental Committee on Sterilization*. London: HMSO.

10. DAWTRY, F. (ed.) (1968). *Social Problems of Drug Abuse*. London: Butterworth.

11. EDITORIAL (1966). *Br. med. J.* **2**, 1553.

12. HAYTER, A. (1968). *Opium and the Romantic Imagination*. London: Faber.

13. HOME OFFICE (1968). *Cannabis*. Report by the Advisory Committee on Drug Dependence. (Chairman: Sir Edward Wayne.) London: HMSO.

14. HOME OFFICE (1968). *Powers of Arrest and Search in Relation to Drug Offences*. Report by the Advisory Committee on Drug Dependence. (Chairman: Sir Edward Wayne.) London: HMSO.

15. LEIGH V. GLADSTONE [1909]. 26 T.L.R. 139. D.C.

16. MINISTRY OF HEALTH (1961). *Leucotomy in England and Wales, 1942–1945*. Reports on Public Health and Medical Subjects, No. 104. London: HMSO.

17. RADCLIFFE, C. J. (1960). *The Law and Its Compass*. London: Faber.

18. R. V. ADAMS [1957]. Unreported.

19. R. V. BOURNE [1939]. 1 K.B. 687.

20. R. V. CONEY [1882]. 8 Q.B.D. 534.

21. R. V. COWBURN (1959). *Crim. Law Rev.* 590, C.C.A.

22. R. V. DONOVAN [1934]. 2 K.B. 498, C.C.A.

23. R. V. PREVOST (1965). 109 S.J. 738.

24. R. V. SMITH (1966). *Crim. Law Rev.* 588, C.C.A.

25. R. V. WARNER [1968]. 2 W.L.R. 1303, H.L.

26. YEANDEL V. FISHER [1966]. 1 Q.B. 440, C.A.

11: Drugs and the Role of the Doctor

R. M. HARE

MY remarks in this paper will fall into two parts. Both of these bear on matters which we have discussed in this group, and I think they severally and jointly illustrate the principles on which the moral questions arising in all these fields ought to be dealt with. I shall discuss, first, the morality of drug taking by individuals, confining myself to drugs in the sense of 'dope'. And after that I shall discuss how a medical man can, in principle, set about deciding what his duty is in dealing with this and other problems. I shall not include any theoretical philosophy. I have a theoretical position in moral philosophy with which some philosophers will disagree. I shall not try to defend this here but shall apply it to these practical problems in the hope that it may shed light on them. If the theory is mistaken, then the light is an *ignis fatuus*; but I am confident enough in it to think it worth-while to see how it works out in practice.

First, I must explain very summarily what the theory is. It is, like all ethical theories, a theory about the meaning of the moral words ('ought' and so on), and the nature of the moral concepts. It is a theory about what we are asking when we ask questions like "What ought I to do in this case?" (where these are moral questions). If we were clear about the meaning of this question this would be a big step towards answering it and, conversely, if we are not clear what it means (and can we honestly say that we are?) this is a great obstacle to even starting to answer it. The answer I would give to the question "What does the question 'What ought I to do in this case?' mean?" is this: what it means is to be explained (like the meaning of any other utterance) by saying what the utterer is doing in uttering it. In the case of a question, obviously, what he is doing is asking something. Asking a question is one species of the genus 'asking for something'; it is that species in which what is asked for is an answer. So we can say what he is doing in asking "What ought I to do in this case?" by finding out for what kind of answer he is asking—in other words, what would constitute an answer to his question. The answer to the question "What ought I to do in this case?" is what some philosophers call a prescription—using the word in a sense somewhat more general than, but otherwise not different from, the sense in which doctors use it: something which tells either what we are to, or what we ought to, do in this case. The answer is not, however, *any* kind of prescription. What makes the word 'ought' appropriate rather than merely the imperative 'are to do' is the fact that moral prescriptions have to be (as philosophers say) universalizable; that is, in giving a moral prescription we are saying (by implication) not merely that such-and-such ought to be done in this case, but that the same thing ought to be done in any case resembling this case either exactly or in the relevant particulars. This logical feature of the word 'ought' is, as we shall see, extremely important for moral reasoning.

So, in asking "What ought I to do in this case?" we are asking for a universal prescription for cases like this. To accept a certain answer to it is to accept a universal principle applicable to all cases like this— whether, in the other cases, it is I that occupy the role in them that I do in this case, or whether it is somebody else and I occupy some other role. It would take too long to go into all the complications and possible misunderstandings that can arise in connexion with this interpretation of moral questions. Perhaps the matter will become clearer when I come to apply the theory to actual examples.

Let us then ask what is wrong about taking certain drugs, and how we can answer the question whether to take a certain drug in certain circumstances is wrong. I shall confine myself to the question of whether it is morally wrong. That it is nearly always extremely unwise or imprudent to start taking, for example, heroin hardly needs to be argued. But there is also the question whether it is morally wrong, and this might be asked even in cases where there was no question of imprudence— that is, even in cases in which it could be established that the pleasure gained by taking, say, cannabis amply compensated for any harm it did to the taker. Before I leave the question of whether certain drugs are harmful, I must point out that the answer is going to be extremely relevant to some moral questions—namely, questions about the morality of putting drugs into the hands of other people. Even if it were agreed that a man who did harm to himself by taking a certain drug was not thereby doing anything morally wrong (merely being unwise or imprudent), it would still be the case that a man who did the same sort of harm to somebody else by giving him the same drug would be doing something morally wrong, for reasons which I hope to elucidate shortly.

Let us start with a simplified artificial example. There are four families on a small island and the island is pretty inhospitable. Hard work by all in farming and fishing is required if they are not to starve. The father of one family, instead of growing potatoes in one small part of his plot, grows cannabis and having prepared the resin smokes it contentedly all day instead of looking after his farm. His land gets covered with weeds and pests which spread to his neighbours' land; his family do what they can to keep up the food supply and, because they are indulgent, they give the father an equal share of what there is; but the whole family is brought below the subsistence level and the children are saved from getting deficiency diseases only by the kindness and charity of the neighbours from whom they go round begging. We have to ask: "Could such a man be doing what he morally ought not to do, although he himself is better off doing it than not doing it?" Let us say that the pleasure he gets from smoking cannabis more than compensates for any harm he suffers—perhaps his appetite is reduced so that he doesn't feel hungry—and, even if he dies earlier than he would have otherwise, the life of a cannabis smoker is so much preferable to facing the rigours of life on the island unaided that, on balance, he has done the best for himself.

This example is over-simplified but it will suffice to illustrate the application of my theory. If there are difficulties with the example because of disagreement about the actual effects of cannabis, it does not matter. The name of any other drug that would have the effects I have described can be substituted. I am not discussing, let alone attacking, cannabis in particular. I am describing a possible experiment which we could, if it were not unethical, try out with *any* drug to determine whether it would be wrong to take it in the situation described. We would put a group of families on a rather infertile island, allow only one of the fathers to take the drug, and observe the effects. It would even be instructive to work out what would be the effects of his taking some imaginary drug, not yet invented, with certain pharmacological properties. So let us imagine that some drug is invented which would have the effects described and that we are assessing the morality of taking it.

I now ask what, if anything, is wrong about the man's action in taking the drug. The answer is that if we put ourselves in his place, and ask "What universal principle can I accept for people in just my position?" the answer is unlikely to be "Grow and take the drug." He has only to consider the effects of his taking it on others—for example, on his children. Although he may be perfectly ready to accept the *singular* prescription that *he* should take the drug, he will not, if he thinks about the matter, accept the universal prescription that *anybody* in his position should take it even if he himself is not in the position of being affected adversely in the way that his children are. To put it more concretely: can he prescribe that his own father should have acted in this way when he (the man on the island) was a child?

Suppose that, when faced with the question "What universal prescription can you accept?" he says: "I can accept the prescription that anybody who wants to should grow and take cannabis. For even if the drug does lead to a lessening of effort so that if everyone takes it the whole island will fall below the subsistence level, the pleasure to be had from the drug will compensate us for this. Better to anaesthetize ourselves against the evils of life than to try to face them. I can put myself imaginatively in the position of anybody (even the children) affected by the general adoption of such a way of life and still recommend it." This answer ought not to satisfy us. For the question is not how he, with his temperament and inclinations, likes the prospect of an island in which everyone takes cannabis. It is, rather, a question of what other people, given their temperaments and inclinations, would suffer if their whole way of life were changed in this way.

The maxim "As ye would that men should do to you, do ye also to them likewise" is frequently misinterpreted owing to a peculiarity of English syntax. The Greek means, literally, "As you wish that men should do" (*kathōs thelete* (indicative) *hina poiōsin*). This point has escaped the translators of the *New English Bible*. The question is not "What would I wish (with my temperament, and so on) if I were in their position?" but rather "What *do* I wish *should* be done to me if I were in their position (with *their* temperaments)?" It is their wishes that I have to consider, not the wishes that I would have (being the sort of man that I am) if *I* were in their position. The wishes are, in fact, part of the other man's shoes into which I have to put myself.

So our drug-taker, if he wants to stick it out, is faced with the following choice. He has to say he is willing that, if he were in the positions of the rest of the people in his society, he should have *either* to let his whole way of life be eroded by the general taking of the drug, *or* to work harder himself in order to make good the supply of food which is being lost by the idleness of those who are taking the drug.

To this I can see only one obvious answer. This is for the drug-taker to say "I am content that the few people who *want* to take the drug should take it; these will be few, and the rest—good, hard-working, abstemious fellows—can always carry them on their back without really noticing it." This makes the argument comparable to the following: "It is all right for me to pick the primroses when I go for a walk in the woods because not many people want to pick primroses, and if everyone who *wants* to pick them does so there will still be plenty left for the others to look at; although if *everyone* went and picked the primroses in the woods there wouldn't be any primroses left, or perhaps even any woods. So I am able to prescribe universally that *those who want to* should pick them, although I am not able to prescribe universally that *everybody* should pick them." Such a man is still prescribing that *everyone in his position* should do the act proposed; only his position includes the fact that he, and not many others, want to do it. This is what differentiates the 'primrose' case from another case that is often quoted in the philosophical literature—in which a man is able covertly to water his garden from the mains when there is a drought and a ban on such use of mains water. This man cannot prescribe that those who want to use water should use it, because nearly everyone who has a garden wants to use it and if they all did there would not be enough water to drink.

Whether the 'cannabis' case is like the 'primrose' case or like the 'water' case (and therefore whether the answer I have put into the mouth of the cannabis-smoker will do) depends on the empirical question: How many people in such a situation would want to take cannabis if it were available and would they take enough to incapacitate themselves for work? This is really the kind of question that pharmacologists, psychologists and sociologists have to answer (only for our more complex society instead of for the tight little island I have described). They have to say just how much of a burden, if any, the taking of a particular drug by individuals imposes on society. If the burden is great enough for us to say that the drug-takers are parasites on society, then not only can we condemn their behaviour but we can legitimately take steps to prevent the habit spreading (though this is not established by the argument I have set out so far; the step from moral condemnation to legal prohibition requires additional justification).

The basis of the whole argument is really that a man cannot say that it is right for him to do something that he is not willing that everybody in his position should do. If he wants to claim that it is right for him to do something that he is not willing that everybody should do, he has to show that there is something special about his position which other people do not share. Privilege, in fact, has to be justified.

I now come to my second question—an entirely different one—about the duties of doctors. This is a much more general question. We have discussed in this group not only the question of how medical men can best help the drug addict, but also questions about brain surgery and castration. I shall not deal with these questions individually and in detail. The details are, of course, the source of most of our difficulties with these problems but as a philosopher I am not competent to discuss them. I want to make the only helpful contribution that I can, which is to set out what I think are the general lines on which such problems can be dealt with.

How does a doctor set about answering the question "What ought I to do to this patient?" In the great majority of cases, no philosophical difficulties arise. The doctor has no doubt about the purposes he is trying to further by the use of his skill: they are the survival and freedom from pain and disability of the patient. Because these are the only or by far the most important purposes that he, as a doctor, has, and because the question of how to attain them is a medical not a philosophical one, the medical man does not in these cases need to philosophize. The cases which cause him to philosophize are cases where these purposes conflict, either with each other or with other purposes which seem of great importance. For example, in some cases where abortion is in question,

89

the doctor might be said to have two patients the survival of both of whom cannot be ensured. In other cases the survival of a patient can be had at the cost of leaving him in severe pain or in some way permanently disabled; or, as with leucotomy in some cases, one disability may be removed at the cost of a different disability—or at least a change in personality which some might count as a disability. In other cases, again, there is the possibility of ensuring a patient's survival by a transplant, but at enormous expense which the patient cannot meet so that it falls on society. How does the surgeon balance the benefit to the patient against the cost to the Treasury? In other cases still, by inflicting a fairly small harm on the patient (for example by castration or by confining him in a mental hospital) he can be prevented from inflicting very great harm on other members of society. These are the sorts of cases that make doctors ask philosophers how to answer the moral questions that arise.

I think that the very general account which I gave earlier of the meaning of the moral words and the logic of moral reasoning which this meaning generates can be applied as it stands to these medical cases. It is, in fact, the basis of all moral reasoning. Let me start with cases in which only one person—the patient—is concerned, and the choice is between his death and his survival with his brain very gravely damaged (say after resuscitation by heart massage). Briefly, if the doctor asks himself, as he must in all such moral dilemmas "What can I prescribe to be done in any case just like this—what, for example, if the patient were myself, only with this man's prospects and desires?" his answer will depend on what he thinks is best for the patient, from the patient's own point of view. I do not think that this way of putting the question sets an insoluble problem for doctors. They have to exercise a sympathetic understanding of the patient's position; and in my experience doctors are better at this than most people.

Much more difficult are cases in which the doctor's action affects more than one person. Normally one of these will be his patient and the others not. Are we to say that the doctor's sole duty is to his patient and he can forget about the interests of the others? Can we say this, even when we are speaking only of his duty *qua* doctor? For of course he may have duties in virtue of other roles which he simultaneously plays, such as that of public employee—he may have a duty not to confer some minor benefit on his patient at a vast cost to the Health Service. But, in any case, what do we mean when we speak of people having duties *qua* this or that or in virtue of roles that they play?

Let us suppose that a doctor can save the life of an old and not particularly happy invalid who will then be an almost insupportable burden to his family. Most of us, I think, would say that he should act in the interest of his patient, the invalid, and put this above the interests of the family. Why do we say this? We evidently think that the doctor has a peculiar duty to his patient. But not to do *anything*. If it were in the patient's interest that some other person should be poisoned, we would not say that the doctor because of his peculiar duty to his patient, should exercise his skill in this way.

At first sight it may seem as if our belief that a doctor has a peculiar duty to his patient runs counter to the method of moral argument that I have been advocating. For this method demands that no differentiation be made between cases simply on the ground that different *individuals* play different roles in them; moral differences can only arise because of differences in the *properties* of the individuals occupying the different roles. This is the consequence of the form of the moral question. We have put it in the form "What can you prescribe universally for cases which are just like this (that is, which have all the same properties as this) no matter what individuals occupy the different roles?" It might therefore be thought that a doctor cannot say that he has a duty to do something for his patient but does not have a duty to do the same thing for the man in the next bed with the same disease who is not his patient but the patient of some other doctor.

This, however, is a misunderstanding. The duty of a doctor to his patient is grounded in the relational property in which that patient stands to him, and in which the other man does not stand, viz., the property of being his patient. I have, similarly, duties to my wife, because she is my wife, which I would not have to her twin sister if she had one, however alike they are. These are duties which *anybody* (at least if his situation is like mine in the relevant or in all respects) has to *his* wife.

So, then, we are allowed to say that a doctor has duties to his patient in virtue of the peculiar relation in which they stand to one another. This differentiates the patient from otherwise similar men. And there is another thing that differentiates the doctor from other men: his medical skill. 'Ought' implies 'can'. So the fact that a layman cannot heal a patient means that he has no duty to do so; this duty is incurred by the doctor because he has the skill to fulfil it. Thus the peculiar duties of the doctor are founded upon these two things—his special skill and his special relation to the patient.

The universal prescription which I find myself able to accept as governing the actions of doctors *qua* doctors is the following: that doctors should use their special skill to further those interests of their own patients which are concerned with the patients' survival, and freedom from pain and disability, balancing these interests against one another so as to promote the overall interest of the patient as best they know. I have no time to justify my acceptance of this prescription; this would take a lot of examination. Nor shall I have time to ask what qualifications and additions are necessary to it. I offer it as a first attempt only.

This, however, is only the doctors' duty *qua* doctors. I mentioned that they might also have a duty *qua* public servants, to exercise reasonable economy. And they have other duties too. Among these are duties to the other people more or less directly affected by their actions. For example, the case of the family of the invalid, mentioned earlier; the much discussed matter of whether a doctor can take into account the interests of the other children when deciding whether to terminate a pregnancy; and the case of the mental patient who has to be locked up in the interests of other people. I would hold that these duties to others could in principle override the doctor's duty to promote the interests of his patient. That is to say, I could myself in principle accept some universal prescriptions (even treating the interests of all the parties to a situation as of equal weight with my own interests) which would allow a doctor to put the greater interests of some other person or of society above the lesser interests of his patient. I say that I could accept such universal prescriptions in principle. But cases in which they would apply are likely to be rare in practice, apart from certain well-defined and easily statable exceptions which can be incorporated into the principle, like that about locking up madmen.

Doctors would therefore do well, having adopted some fairly simple set of principles which copes adequately with the cases they are likely to meet, to dismiss from their minds (at least when they are doctoring) the possibility of there being further exceptions to their principles. For doctors, like all of us, are human, and if they once start thinking, when engaged on a case, that this case may be one of a limitless and indeterminate set of exceptions to their principles, they will find such exceptions everywhere. There may be—in fact there certainly are—cases in which soldiers ought to run away in battle. But if soldiers were all the time asking themselves whether the particular battle in which they were fighting might be such a case, they would all run away every time. The temptation to special pleading is too great. A doctor once said to me, in connexion with the proposal to allow euthanasia: "We shall start by putting patients away because they are in intolerable pain and haven't long to live anyway; and we shall end up by putting them away because it's Friday night and we want to get away for the weekend."

I think that if doctors form for themselves very firm and fairly simple principles in matters of this sort, and do not question them, this will lead in practice to as great a proportion of right decisions as can be expected. That doctors should think in this way is what I find myself able to prescribe universally, though I have not time to justify my prescription. I think that the exceptions, if there are any, do not need to be looked for; if there are any, and we come across them, they will force themselves on our attention.

12: Some Philosophical Comments

B. G. MITCHELL and R. M. HARE

IN these comments I shall examine what might be called the 'citadel' view of a man's personality, because it seems to me that this sort of view determines our attitude to the use of scientific techniques for modifying personality.

On one of the central issues Professor Hare has commented (personal communication) that some of the torment that such (moral) questions commonly cause in those who have to answer them arises from a desire to preserve a strict line of demarcation between a man's personality (his soul or citadel, which ought not to be tampered with) and his circumstances or environment (which may be altered without giving rise to such difficult problems). Professor Hare believes that this citadel view is untenable and that the problems are best approached in terms of a man's interests. He suggests that we should set the same limits on tampering with a man's personality as we should on tampering with anything else that powerfully affects his interests.

A powerful illustration of a scientific technique which modifies personality is the technique of brainwashing. If I become a prisoner of war in the hands of the Chinese I may, by deprivation of sleep and by long interrogations, be brought to a condition in which I totally abandon my present system of values and embrace those of Chairman Mao. I shall have become a fanatic whose attitudes and beliefs are totally repugnant to the man I was before, and this will have happened as a result of processes beyond my conscious control, indeed against such resistance as I was able to offer. This is the most complete assault on my personality that can be conceived and the citadel metaphor is the natural one to use. The citadel of my personality has been systematically demolished and reconstructed on a plan to which I am, or was, totally opposed.

Compare with this castration or hormone treatment or aversion therapy undertaken at the patient's request in order to enable him to control impulses which are otherwise impossible or abnormally difficult for him to master. Examples of such impulses might be an inordinate or deviant sexual urge or a habit of physiological or psychological dependence on some drug. In such a case the individual's system of values is not under attack. He is asking for treatment which will restore to him the degree of freedom in conducting his life which is enjoyed by normal people whose appetites are manageable. It is as if the citadel of his soul had been under siege and he had asked for and obtained relief.

From a citadel point of view brainwashing is totally objectionable and these other treatments almost entirely unobjectionable. There are obvious disadvantages to the individual in being deprived of his reproductive capacities and in having to undergo treatment which is in itself unpleasant, and these must be given some weight. They are, however, interferences with his personality only in so far as they deprive him of certain ways of expressing his personality or take certain matters out of the control of his will. This suggests, what is in any case obvious enough, that the effect on the patient's personality is only one of the factors to be borne in mind. *Other things being equal* one would not be justified in tampering with someone's personality, but there are cases in which other things are far from equal.

Such cases are those for whom leucotomy is offered as a remedy. It is only in the case of severe mental illness and/or intense and continuous distress that such a remedy would be contemplated. Dr Tredgold (p. 45) has carefully assessed the sort of considerations involved. Interestingly, he seems to take the citadel view for granted. In considering whether as a result of the operation personality damage had occurred he writes (p. 47): "Many patients were happier, showed no loss of moral, intellectual or aesthetic standards and seemed to be their old selves, freed from a terrible illness." In other patients in Dr Tredgold's series it seemed to be more difficult to tell whether deterioration had occurred. In some there was reported ". . . a reduction of standards, a release of hostility and a lack of consideration." (p. 47).

Prima facie, then, these were cases of personality damage. Some psychiatrists associate personality damage very closely with loss of moral, intellectual or aesthetic standards, and I agree with this. But they also recognize that an individual's standards may be morbidly exaggerated, which perhaps suggests that the man's standards are in some way not fully his own. Where this is the case, release of hostility and egocentric behaviour may be a necessary step to more mature development. When this happens it is tempting to say that the man himself is imprisoned in his own citadel and this temptation is enough to show that the citadel analogy is somewhat too crude.

No doubt a man may be involved in such intense suffering that it must be relieved even at the cost of some impairment of his personality, or the higher capacities of the personality may be so distorted that it is better to weaken them altogether than to leave them in their present state. The victim of a tyrannical conscience would be better off less conscientious. But, although they may sometimes be justifiably overridden, the claims of personality are always of the greatest importance.

94

The 'cash value' of the citadel view would, then, be something like this. A man's moral, intellectual and aesthetic standards, in so far as they are genuinely his, are to be identified more closely with the man himself than are his other desires and interests, since the latter could be altered without making him a markedly different sort of man. This seems to involve certain judgments of value or at any rate of importance, because when I say 'a markedly different sort of man' I primarily mean 'a man different in certain important respects'.

Before attempting the difficult task of making this conception more precise, I shall cite one more example of the effect a scientific technique may have on personality, that is, the effect of psychoanalysis on religious faith. It has been suggested that in some way the personality restructuring that goes on during psychoanalysis reduces the need for religion and that, in psychoanalytic terms, religious feeling can be viewed alongside other complex aspects of personality such as deep involvement in music, art, philanthropy, ambitious aims or sociopolitical beliefs. We have already noted that in some mental illnesses conscience may be morbidly increased and presumably religious, artistic, political and other attitudes could be similarly affected. These comments imply that not only morbid but also normal religious feeling is affected by the psychoanalytic process. The question which naturally arises is whether religion is, as such, a morbid phenomenon or whether psychoanalysis must be judged in certain cases to impair the personality. In this connexion we may note that patients often ask for a Christian psychiatrist, presumably as some guarantee against a treatment which will impair their faith.

To return to the citadel view. There are a number of objections to it.

(1) It is too intellectualist. Moral, intellectual and aesthetic standards may be important to intellectuals but not to most people. The things and people that individuals are attached to matter as much to them or more than any standards. This is true. To be brainwashed so that I no longer loved my wife, or even my dog, would be a serious invasion of my personality.

(2) It is too individualist. It suggests that the individual is the master of his fate and captain of his soul to a quite unrealistic extent. It is only within certain limits that I choose to be the person that I am. This also is true, but does not detract from the importance of developing and preserving such powers of self-determination as I have.

(3) It is culture-bound. Lady Barbara Wootton[2] quotes J. C. Moloney on the predicament of the psychoanalyst in Japan. "Should the American and the Japanese psychoanalytic therapist encourage individualism or should they insist upon insensible and unconscious

4*

submissive conformity to the existing culture?... The Japanese psychoanalyst, faced with the problem of curing a mentally ill person, must first of all diagnose him as ill because he does not adhere to the rigidly presented culture patterns I have outlined. The cure upon which the analyst then embarks constitutes the opposite of a cure by Western standards. Instead of endeavouring, as do Occidental psychoanalysts, to free the individual from his inner thongs, the Japanese analyst actually tightens those thongs."

This seems to be the most troublesome objection, because it draws attention to the extent to which our conception of what constitutes normal personality depends on certain value judgments. We admire and encourage free and autonomous personalities in a way the Japanese do not. More awkward still, differences of this kind may be found nearer home. The citadel view until quite recently reflected an ideal of an inner-directed person who reflectively chose his standards and lived in accordance with them, even if this involved conflict with his own desires and with the judgment of others. It set a high value on the individual's conscious control of his impulses, which constituted him a man of principle, or a strong character.

This ideal appears to be increasingly challenged. It represents, in the eyes of many, a positively objectionable type, the authoritarian personality, whose characteristic virtues of discipline and self-control already have an old-fashioned ring. As an ideal and perhaps also in actuality it is being superseded by what Philip Rieff calls the therapeutic personality.[1] He argues that a "revolution is being fought for a permanent disestablishment of any deeply internalized moral demands. . . . The therapy of all therapies is not to attach oneself exclusively to any particular therapy, so that no illusion may survive of some end beyond an intensely private sense of well-being to be generated in the living of life itself."

If there is any truth in this it would explain the conflict of opinion about mood-affecting drugs. From the standpoint of the older soul-citadel view the use of these is objectionable in so far as they deprive the individual temporarily of that conscious power to order his own life which is essential to his being the man he is, and may in the long-term permanently reduce it. He drifts when he ought to steer. But no objection is felt by those who see in it only a harmless means of enlarging their experience and who attach no overriding importance to continuous rational control.

It would seem to follow from this discussion that one's view as to what sorts of scientific interference with personality are legitimate, and even one's view as to what counts as interference with personality, depends on one's view as to what in human personality is important and what kind of human personality is to be valued.

MAN'S INTERESTS: R. M. HARE

Professor Mitchell explores sympathetically a metaphor—the citadel—which I had rejected as misleading. I still think it is misleading and shall try to explain why. This is not merely because it is a metaphor. On the whole metaphors are to be eschewed in philosophy though they can sometimes, if it is not forgotten that they are only metaphors, be illuminating. What is wrong with this one is that it can be cashed in two quite distinct ways, between which Professor Mitchell does not distinguish, and thus it remains unclear just what constitutes the sort of assault (on the citadel of the personality) which is to be condemned.

To illustrate these two different ways of cashing the metaphor, consider the contrast which he draws between brainwashing and therapeutic castration. He cites cases in which the brainwashing is done without the victim's consent but in which the castration is done with the patient's consent. This makes it look as if the assault on the personality consists in acting without the consent of the patient. Professor Mitchell comments on the example he gives of brainwashing that it is done "as a result of processes beyond my conscious control, indeed against such resistance as I was able to offer" (p. 93). And he describes the therapeutic castration as being done at the patient's request. But it is obvious that the distinction between personality changes brought about with, and those brought about without, the patient's consent is an entirely different distinction from that between changes in the personality and changes which do not amount to changes in the personality. For one could bring about very radical changes in the personality with the patient's consent, or one could bring about changes in matters not affecting his personality without his consent. The two distinctions are therefore independent. I hope that Professor Mitchell, who fails to keep them separate, has not thereby been led to think that, in recommending that we abandon the metaphor of the soul-citadel, I am recommending that we dismiss as unimportant the distinction between operations with and without consent.

This latter distinction is certainly a difficult one—there are awkward borderline cases—but for all that it is surely fundamental. So I shall take *this* distinction for granted (I shall say more later about the reasons for its importance) and concentrate on the alleged other distinction, that between what is inside and what is outside the citadel of the personality. In discussing castration or brainwashing, for example, I shall not consider whether they are done with or without the patient's consent, taking it for granted that there are very good moral reasons in nearly all cases for condemning such things if done without consent. I shall ask, rather, whether, if they are done *with* the consent of the patient, the concept of a soul-citadel is a helpful one in deciding when we ought and when we ought not to do them.

It would be easier to discuss this question if the upholders of the soul-citadel view gave a clear statement of what we are to count as an invasion of the citadel. The comment that Dr Tredgold seems to take a citadel view for granted is not supported by the passages that are quoted. The alteration, whether beneficial or the reverse, of the patient's standards are noted and I agree that a man's moral, intellectual and aesthetic standards form an important part of his personality, although (for reasons which Professor Mitchell gives) not the whole of it. But I find nothing here to support the view that the line between what we can and what we cannot justifiably do to a patient is coincident with a line between interference with and non-interference with his personality, even if the latter expression has been clarified (though also over-simplified) by equating it with the patient's values. Professor Mitchell himself says that the citadel analogy is too crude.

The matter becomes much clearer if we abandon the analogy of the *citadel* and talk instead in terms of the patient's *interests*, which can be more or less radically affected either by changes in his personality or values, or by changes in his physical state or environment. In these terms we can easily see that there is a presumption, though only a presumption, that changes in a man's values will be radically against his interests. This is because values are one important kind of interest. If I were told that by a simple treatment my enjoyment of music, which I now very much enjoy, would be stopped, I should regard this as an attack on my interests which I ought to resist with all my power. But suppose that instead of this I were told that by an equally simple treatment I should be made to like music, I having until now been entirely unmusical. This too would be a change in my values; but I should be inclined to go ahead with this treatment, even if I knew that as a result I should come to dislike very much some things that I now do not mind at all, such as hearing my neighbour sing out of tune in his bath.

What these examples seem to show is that changes in a person's values are not automatically against his interests and therefore not auto-matically objectionable. However, my present values are often, indeed usually, something by which I set great store.

Contrast the hypothetical case where what I enjoy is not music but the sexual satisfaction which, for me, is only to be had by strangling little girls. That I enjoy this is also part of my values; and I suppose that those who think that my values are what constitute my personality might say that if an operation took away from me this enjoyment, and the desire for it, it would have altered my personality. But I might very much want this to happen, either because I had a moral repugnance to what the pursuit of this desire would make me do, or because I was simply afraid of what the law would do to me (that is, keep me incarcerated in an institution). The considerations involved here are all considerations about my interests and, of course, the interests of the little girls. The question of whether the operation would be invading a citadel is not a helpful one to ask.

We can best understand such cases, and decide what we ought to do in them, by imagining that we ourselves were the man who was to have the operation. What do we think should be done then, if our case were just like this man's? Of course we must not read our own present desires or values into the mind of the man we are considering; for his will no doubt be different and it is his that matter since it is his interests that we are supposed to be considering. But we are to give weight to his desires and his interests as if they were our own (not, however, forgetting the others whom his actions may affect, to whose interests we must also give the same weight).

When we come to the leucotomy cases the same considerations apply. We find a man with a certain personality, a certain set of values, and also certain psychological handicaps which it would be unreal to separate from his personality. He is that sort of man—perhaps he was not always so over-anxious or so abnormally quick-tempered—but that is the sort of man he is now. If the handicaps are so distressing that he wants to be relieved of them even at the cost of becoming a different sort of person, then this is a sign that it may be in his interest to bring this about. And that is what we have to consider.

It will be asked how we decide what is in his interest. It is because we find it so difficult to decide this for somebody else that we lay such stress on obtaining his consent. It is hard for us to imagine ourselves into his position, which may be quite unlike our own; and therefore, if we can ask him, it is best to let him decide in his own interest. But there are limitations to this. It is hard for *him* to imagine what it will be like for him after the operation—which he has to do if he is to make an informed choice. We may therefore have to try to explain this to him, using our knowledge of other cases. Or he may be so disturbed that he cannot give us an answer which we feel represents what he would decide if he were not disturbed. Or he may just be unconscious. Here we have to start guessing—perhaps asking those who know him well, perhaps generalizing from what most people would want, perhaps even asking what *we* would want or what we would be glad to have had done to us, after the operation was over. But we must avoid the danger, inherent in the last question, of trying to fashion this man after *our* idea of what a man ought to be. For it is his interests and not our ideals that are in question. Even if after the process (be it brainwashing or an operation or a combination of both) he came to accept our ideals and repudiate his previous ones, we should have done violence to his interests unless we were absolutely sure that this was what, before we did it, he wanted.

It is in this consideration of other people's interests, and the refusal to impose upon them our own ideals, that real respect for people's personality lies—a respect which the citadel metaphor only makes needlessly mysterious.

CITADEL VERSUS INTERESTS

Mitchell and *Hare* discussed the points of difference in their respective *Philosophical Comments*, *Mitchell* defending his use of *the citadel* (it now looks too static in view of the *Chairman's* presentation of a dynamic concept of personality [p. 128]), and *Hare* defending his formula of *interests*.

Mitchell: I accept your criticism that I have not distinguished between compulsion and voluntary acceptance of treatment, but this omission does not seriously affect my argument. Even if a man consented to what amounted to an invasion of his citadel this would still not be enough to justify it.

Hare: I would suggest three interpretations of the citadel metaphor: (*a*) acting against a man's express wish (but this does not answer the question, 'what may I do to a man with his consent?'); (*b*) altering a man's values fundamentally (this is against *his interests* in nearly all cases, but can be tested by asking the question, 'what, if it were I, would I have done to me?'); and (*c*) the impairment of a man's freedom to determine his own decisions (a new interpretation, not introduced until now).

Mitchell: Surely these three interpretations are unified by a conception of personality in terms of which people ought to take responsibility for their lives, that is, act in accordance with the values in which they believe. Personality would be impaired if values were altered otherwise than by persuasion or if the ability for self-determination were reduced.

Hare: I agree that all this would be against a person's interests.

Mitchell: But it would not be against his interests unless it were supposed that he would be in some way a more complete person had he not been interfered with; behind the concept of interests is a concept of what a fully developed personality would be like.

Hare: 'A man's interest' is a compendious term for what a man would want if . . . etc.—a very complex notion. For the practising doctor the matter is simpler than it appears when one talks about personality.

Mitchell: Can we take the example of a hypothetical non-addictive drug which permanently makes the taker more contented with life and less capable of using his talents? Suppose someone wished to take the drug. Would it be acting in his interest for another person to offer it to him?

Hare: Yes, but if the drug were distributed widely it would prove to be against the general interest. The case against such drugs is that they harm society.

Mitchell: So the difference is clear. In your view the only objection to such drugs is the social one. In my view there is another objection—they might induce self-imposed impairment of capacities and, therefore, of personality.

Hare: It is misleading to use the citadel model for this because we are now talking about what a man should be—a different question. You and I would abhor the offer of such a drug because we think a man should not be the sort of man which the drug would make him.

Mitchell: Quite so. In saying that we do not want him to become that sort of person, we mean we want him to continue to be a self-directing personality with a clear sense of values, that is, to have a citadel.

Hare: We share the idea of what a person ought to be. We differ in our views of how far it is right to impose our ideas on other people.

REFERENCES

1. RIEFF, P. (1965). In *Triumph of the Therapeutic: Uses of Faith after Freud*, pp. 240, 261. New York: Torchbooks, Harper and Row.
2. WOOTTON, B. (1959). In *Social Science and Social Pathology*, p. 210. New York: Humanities Press.

13: Authority and Personality in the Christian Tradition

G. R. DUNSTAN

AT a time when strong emotional attitudes are widely held and publicly argued, common responses are of two sorts. The first is to interpret previous tradition in terms of the contemporary clue or slogan, for example, 'existential relationships', 'permissiveness', 'openness'. The second is to react negatively and to emphasize the contrary elements in the tradition, for example, the paternalist, the authoritarian, the conventional. If I avow my own bias towards the second of these ways, it is not because I claim for it an essential superiority, but simply in order that it may be declared and allowance made for it in what I write. And since the material with which the theologian has principally to work is the highly symbolic language of the biblical tradition and its varied formulations in the theological tradition, the risk of partiality in interpretation is high. A full study of my subject would require a detailed analysis of the traditions of both moral and ascetic theology. In this paper I can only offer some general clues.

On the west front of Bath Abbey there are carved two ladders (*scalae*) with figures on them. They are commonly taken to be Jacob's ladder, but they are not. They represent a dream of Oliver King, Bishop of Bath and Wells from 1495 to 1504, whose motto, *de sursum est ut discam*, is depicted on the walls of his chantry chapel in St George's Chapel, Windsor Castle, where he was once a canon. The ladders may be taken as a symbol of the two scales with which the theologian has to reckon in answering the questions put to him, the time-scale (*scala saeculorum*) against which he holds that revelation has occurred, and the scale of perfection (*scala perfectionis*) by which man has made and measured his ascent to the vision of God.

In the Judaeo–Christian tradition the self-disclosure of God, and the disclosing to man of man himself and of the truth and falsehood of his relationships, has been made through history. In a series of events, traced in the biblical literature from the call of Abraham, to the death and resurrection of Jesus and the consequent mission of the Church, these disclosures have been made, and men responding to them have been committed to certain religious and moral obligations arising from what they have seen. Notionally it would be easier if we could plot these disclosures neatly on the time-scale, give them dates and find in them a logically or emotionally satisfying development, for example, from the 'primitive' and wrathful God of the earliest Old Testament to the loving and humanitarian Jesus of the Sermon on the Mount. In fact this has been done so neatly and so often as to leave us with little respect for the attempt. The figures on the time scale are not fixed: they move.

We may consider, for instance, only two of the ways in which the formative event of Hebrew history, the Exodus from Egypt, came to be regarded in Hebrew theology. The rescue of the Israelites from Pharaoh and the Egyptians is presented in the narrative as a paternalistic, authoritarian act of a mighty and powerful God: God brought 'his son' out of Egypt with a high hand and led him into the wilderness of Sinai and thence into Canaan, the promised land. But when the prophets look back to those events they write of them differently. Israel is no longer a son but 'the virgin daughter of Israel'. God is no longer the irresistible Father but a suitor, choosing and wooing Israel for his bride. *Ducam eam in solitudinem et loquar ad cor ejus*, said Hosea in the name of God, in a moment of pathetic appeal to Israel, now a faithless and adulterous wife: I will take her back to the desert again, the old trysting-place, and woo her again with words whispered to the heart. Jeremiah took the point, and in a few words (Jeremiah 31, 31–40) on which the whole of Biblical theology turns as on a pivot, describes the new relationship in terms not of the absolute submission which a son would owe to such a father, but of a *covenant*, a marriage covenant, within which husband and wife may reason together, and plead and agree, sorrow and rejoice. Old Testament history and liturgy were rewritten in terms of covenant. The Book of Deuteronomy is a characteristic exposition of it. The covenant relationship was no less demanding than the paternalist one; whether as father or as husband God was not one to be trifled with. But the point of the narration is that, within the Old Testament itself, both interpretations are read into the same event—or, if it be preferred, both disclosures were made through it. Both patterns of relationship move across the scale—with several others—inviting their characteristic responses. There is no neat progression from the submissive response characteristic of the paternalist relation to the response of mutuality implied in the covenant relation. One is not outgrown in favour of the other. Both are available in case of need.

The same double pattern could be derived from the presentation of Jesus in the Gospels and in the Epistles, and by a similar process of simplification. There is no doubt that the most frequent image which Jesus used was that of the Father. It was this relationship which meant most to him, and his filial responses cover the whole range, the scale. There is the element of childlike trust, imposed in one whose love, goodness and providence are not doubted. There is also its corollary, total, absolute obedience. There is certainty about what *is* the Father's will and this dictates its own unambiguous demand: do it. Jesus 'taught with authority', not on what the Law, or convention, or necessity, or the good of society, or the national interest required, but on simply what 'the Father's will' was and demanded. In the Epistles His death is presented as an act of obedience, total and complete. It is true that much of the narrative that we have in the Gospels is shaped by controversy, that between the infant Church and the Jewish Community as well as—and perhaps heightening—that between Jesus and the scribes and Pharisees. But, allowance having been made for this, the portrait of Jesus as a highly authoritarian figure cannot be eliminated: authoritarian in controversy, authoritarian in teaching and in demand. The *method* of parable, aphorism and so on is deceptive. Of the *substance* there is no doubt; it is characterized by the much-used phrase, 'Verily, verily I say unto you'. The Law (which was taken to be the Law of God) might say one thing, 'But *I* say unto you' something else. I do not think we do justice to the Gospels' portrait of Jesus if we explain 'he taught them as having authority' (Mark 1, 22) *merely* in terms of the authoritative, self-authenticating nature of what he taught: the authority of certitude was in himself.

Yet the demand and command are for conditions allowing movement, spontaneity, growth. "Call no man father on earth", He said, to an adult audience, because they had only one Father, even God. This is a call to grow out of dependence on earthly authority. (We are not to be blinded by the contemporary language of 'love' to the fact that it was a Father with authority of whom, as to whom, Jesus spoke.) But the dependence is not passive: it is relational, dynamic, adult. The Father's will is to be *sought, striven for*, as well as done. The righteousness demanded is such as men are to *hunger* and *thirst* after, not such as an easy conformity with the rules can buy. So essential is purity of heart that the eye must be plucked out or the hand or foot cut off if thereby the imagination is to be saved from corruption, and the disposition for all acts be pure. Again, all the art of a great teacher is used to convey this demand, including the awful warning and the use of fear—'Fear not them which kill the body; fear him which has power to cast both soul and body into hell . . .'—but the demand itself is an absolute demand, taught with authority by one who showed no trace of doubt about the message or his duty to pronounce it.

In St Paul all the themes of the past come up again, woven into new patterns by a man who, all his life, was working a new pattern of himself. The authority in St Paul is that of an apostle—the more important to him because disputed—and he does not hesitate to deploy it, against recalcitrant churches and individuals within them, against St Peter himself and, at one time, against the whole apostolic band and the

Church of Jerusalem with it. He is careful to distinguish, as in I Corinthians 7, between his rulings for which he claims 'the word of the Lord', those for which he can claim the custom of the Churches, and those which rest only on his own judgment; but even so he can add that he thinks he has also the Spirit of the Lord on his side. He is a superb casuist, distinguishing for example between occasions when it might be a duty not to eat butcher's meat, because the association of animal slaughter with sacrifice to idols might scandalize tender consciences, and when— no such 'simple believers' being present—it was expedient as well as lawful to eat with a clear conscience. In other words, the notion of complete 'openness', the sense that 'it doesn't matter', was foreign to him: even things indifferent in themselves acquired moral significance in given contexts, even in the context of a man's own conscience or scruple.

Furthermore, facing as he did the problem of integrating predominantly Gentile churches into a Christian community which was in origin Jewish, he was bound to face the major problem of the Jewish law. In this he made two major distinctions. The first is between the ceremonial requirements or 'works' of the Law—those governing circumcision, ritual sacrifice and so on—and the moral requirements, basically the Ten Commandments and rules of a moral and social nature derived from or attending them; the former he declared to be abrogated, the latter to remain in full force. The second distinction was between keeping of the law as a means of acquiring or earning God's favour, and therefore salvation, and keeping it as a dictate of the supreme rule of charity, as a moral consequence of or response to the disclosure of God's own love made in the events concerning Jesus of Nazareth, and as the only requirement consonant with what he regarded as the true nature or life of man. The former—obedience in order to earn grace*— he repudiated, with a vigour which has deceived many every since; the second he fervently upheld. St Paul, rightly understood, never set Law against Love as modern situationists do. Law was to him an expression of love, and a necessary one 'for the hardness of men's hearts'. He would have repudiated antinomianism today as firmly as he renounced it then. But similarly, in his own, finely analysed, moral experience, he knew infallibly that merely to enunciate a law is not to have it obeyed; that even to *want* to keep the law is insufficient. In the self-scrutiny written in Romans 7 he can acquit himself of offences against nine of the commandments but not against the tenth (7, 7f.); the rebellion is in the desire itself, so that it is possible even to desire the highest good for the wrong reason. So he could write the doom of mere moralism—that it is enough to tell people what to do and expect them to do it—in the words 'The good which I would I do not: but the evil

* Calvin was to put the matter succinctly for him centuries later: "The Kingdom of God is not the hire of slaves, but the heritage of sons."

which I would not, that I do' (7, 19). This gap between the will and the accomplishment will appear again in St Augustine.

The methods by which St Paul argued all this were devious. He ranged back and forth along the scale of time, setting Abraham against Moses, and finding the fulfilment of both in Christ. And he ranged far along the scale of perfection, going on from the cathartic analysis of Romans and Galatians—controversial epistles both—to a mature vision of the growth and destiny of human character in Colossians and Ephesians. It is here that we find his dynamic concepts of personality, in the language of 'a full-grown man, the measure of the stature of the fulness of Christ; no longer children, . . . but grown up in all things in him, which is the head, even Christ': and this growth is essentially social, not in isolation as an individual: it is (exploiting the similitude of the body) 'through that which every joint supplieth, according to the working in due measure of each several part, . . . unto the building up of itself in love'. (Ephesians 4, 13–16). To attain this growth no demand was too great, no appeal too strong, no exercise of his apostolic authority *ultra vires*.* An authoritarian proclamation of the events concerning Jesus and of the interpretation built into the narrative of those events, both as he had received them, and an authoritarian demand for a life, corporate in the churches and personal in their members, consonant with that proclamation, with these two together St Paul launched the Church in the West along its way; these were, in fact, the cornerstones of what we once called Christendom. Again, we may wish that the proclamation and the demand were only authoritative, but this would be to ignore what is, surely, an ineradicable element in the portrait.

Between St Paul and St Augustine of Hippo the Church passed through three major formative experiences. One was the necessity to defend, and so (inevitably) to define, its doctrine in a world of rival and eclectic religions pervaded by acute philosophical speculation in the neo-Platonist tradition. In a sense, these were the most gloriously 'open' years of the Church's life until the time of the Scholastic philosophers of the high middle ages. The Fathers were entirely willing to use the philosophy and thought forms of the day in order to express and defend their Gospel— just as St Thomas Aquinas was entirely willing to jettison what to him were their outmoded formulations in order to reinterpret in terms of the rediscovered Aristotelian tradition. But observe: they were open to modes of expression; they were rigid in their defence of a central deposit or pattern of proclamation and moral teaching which was the substance of what they argued about.

* It is true that he can employ the language at least of an appeal to moral reasoning; he does it in a passage fundamental to the Church's later doctrine of natural law, in Romans, chapters 1 and 2; he does it more crisply in I Corinthians—'judge ye what I say'; 'judge ye for yourselves'. but they are only to judge propositions which he has already enunciated; they are not presented with an open situation to be contemplated with open minds.

The second formative experience was official persecution by the Roman State, which produced its own crises, theological as well as ecclesiastical, and which inevitably hardened the hierarchical organization of the Church and its authority. The third experience was the reverse, the growing popularity of Christianity, the coming into the Church of far greater numbers than hitherto it had learned to train in the full demands of its life—a process which was well advanced before the conversion of Constantine and the recognition of Christianity throughout the Empire but which was accelerated by those events. One result of this was to set up a 'desert' Christianity against civic and urban Christianity; to create an ascetic tradition which, though intended primarily for those who embraced the eremitic or coenobitic life, inevitably fed itself back into the married quarters of the Church, the Church of the cities, as men trained in the desert tradition outstripped the rest in stature and became, as bishops, the formative influences in the Church at large. The old discipline of the Church had been hard enough but it was assimilable, for it was a way or style of life held corporately within a community small enough to be, as an Elizabethan divine said marriage ought to be, 'a perpetual friendly fellowship'. The new asceticism was harder in itself. Dogmatically, it owed more to the negative traditions in paganism as well as in Judaism and Christianity, the way of renunciation, and soon it would tend to renounce for unjewish and unchristian reasons, because of a supposed badness in what was renounced instead of a goodness to be set aside for the sake of the highest Good. It had also to be imposed on larger and therefore more impersonal communities. It became part of a penitential discipline, corporate indeed at first, and mercifully intended, but increasingly individualized, formalized, codified, and becoming, at its worst, all that St Paul had repudiated, a Law by which to climb the ladder into heaven.

The major product of these three experiences together was St Augustine of Hippo.[2] He was trapped on the scale of time, caught on the rungs only because he could not let go; for on these rungs he had to struggle for perfection—his own, that of the Church, that of the earthly Empire and all secular rule. We see only a part of this man in the major, methodical treatises, like the *Confessions* and the *City of God*; only an even smaller part in his controversial writings. The major part comes out in his Sermons, in the words uttered daily before his congregations in Hippo but uttered as much to himself as to them.

Dilige, et quod vis fac. The famous words bring us to the heart of the contemporary moral debate, as they take us back to the moral crucifixion of St Paul. *Dilige, et quicquid vis fac*, 'do *everything* that you will', he said in one extension. What did he imply? On the theological time-scale the words take us back to St Paul and the moral scale—the unbridged gap between 'the good that I would' and the poverty of my achievement caused by the defect of desire, the turning of the will from God. There is only one remedy for this: it is the love of God, that is, in the fullness of Johannine theology (and St Augustine was expounding 1 John when he uttered these words), the total response of the human person, affections and will, to the given love of God. Where this is, the gap is bridged; man *can* do what he wills. So: 'Love (*sc.* God), and what you will, do.'

Unfortunately the literature occasioned by this saying[6] will not leave us with so easy a solution, though distinguished Augustinian scholars, like Etienne Gilson, have favoured it. The situationists claim for it a complete validation of their own maxims, seeing in 'love' a power to dispense from every rule. There is material in the context which supports their position. The instances given in the sermon refer more explicitly to the love of neighbour than to the love of God; the illustrations, too, are antithetical—speak or remain silent, punish or spare—suggesting a complete openness to the situation. But the context forbids the claim. Theologically the context is an exposition of 1 John which explicitly derives the love of neighbour from God's love to us, and this must rule out a 'neighbour only' interpretation of the object of *Dilige*. Historically the context is even more shocking. The immediate occasion of the Sermon was criticism, overt or implied, of Augustine's calling-in the Imperial army to defend the Church against a probable victory by the Donatists, themselves an ultra-rigorist sect thrown up by the persecution, and destined to survive for centuries. Is it really right, the objection ran, for Christians to repel Christians, even schismatics, with force of arms, especially the arms of the secular power? Will not your motives be suspect? Even if this *is* right, will it *look* right? The answer came back: *Dilige et quod vis fac*. Make sure that love is in your heart, not rancour; then do what you know you ought to do, without fear either of corruption in yourself or of what men will say of you. *Odium dico dimittas ex corde, non disciplinam*. The argument is similar to that which he used in his requirement of a just war, a war against the Manichees: there must be in the heart of a Christian soldier a real love of the enemy and a hatred of the act of fighting or killing him. 'The real evils of war' (he wrote) are 'not the death of someone who will die in any case' but 'love of violence, revengeful cruelty, fierce and implacable hostility'. Let a disposition of love proof the soldier against these—and he may fight, nay must if the cause be just and authority commands. Thus another of the great formative influences on the Christian moral tradition, even one of its most cryptic and pregnant sayings, was wrought out by historical circumstance, in the life of a man set in a position of authority, wrestling in the same moment with a duty to defend certain truths and an institution to which he was committed and with a duty to advance souls, those in his charge as well as his own, towards a perfection without which the vision of the utterly desired God was unattainable.

It would be tedious, and increasingly inaccurate, to prolong these generalizations through every phase of the Christian tradition. Nevertheless something must be said of the mediaeval and Reformation periods, for the generalizations commonly made about them—describing the first as an age of authority and the second as one, in reaction, of the individual—are both mistaken. There was an increasingly authoritarian element in the mediaeval Western Church as the central government extended its control over doctrinal discussion as well as over the administration of the canon law. But, in these terms, the Reformation was as authoritarian as the age before it. Authority was simply transferred, either to the Prince, as in England and Germany, or to an oligarchy of elders, as in the Calvinist Churches; and both could be as tyrannical as any pope or curia.

Behind the authoritarian front, however, mediaeval Christianity continued a tradition of wide variety and speculation. At different times authority stepped in and gave official and therefore, to some extent, exclusive status to particular theological interpretations. The doctrine of transubstantiation, for instance, was fixed in this way in the thirteenth century. But even the official formulae themselves were patient of wide-ranging speculation. In the suppression of the Albigensians in southern France and of parallel movements in south-east Europe the Church showed itself more forceful, even ruthless, partly because of the overt implications for personal and social morality which these essentially dualist beliefs carried, partly because of political and social complications which encouraged an all-too-ready resort to the sword. The same process was repeated in the suppression of Lollardy in fifteenth-century England and of its contemporary Hussite movements in Bohemia.

Questions of personality and its development, as we ask them now, were not so asked then. Men argued in different terms. In this particular field, orthodoxy would claim to speak with confidence and authority about the 'end' of man's being, that for which he was created, that to which his reason pointed, which was to 'please' God, or to 'see' God, or to 'enjoy' God. In alternative, negative terms, he was to 'flee' or to 'escape' the devil and hell. An essential condition to attain the vision of God was to attain sanctity, the likeness of God. Dogma, again, was confident about what God had already done in Christ to make this possible: every well-appointed Church (Fairford in Gloucestershire, is a superb example) had the Christmas story, the cross of Christ, the harrowing of hell, the resurrection, and the final judgment depicted on its walls, or in its windows, or carved in wood or stone within or without. To doubt this scheme was heresy. This gift of salvation had to be appropriated by man's own effort. The Blessed Virgin Mary and the saints would help him, both by example and by their prayers, but he had to discipline himself also or none of these would avail. Works of mercy or of charity (social benevolence) and works of devotion (religious duties, including adoration, thanksgiving, petition and the sacramental life) were part of his task. So also was the daily discipline of mind and body, necessary because of man's fallen estate: mortification, or the cutting back of overweening desires, the avoiding of the seven deadly sins, the pursuit of the cardinal virtues. On all this the Church taught with confidence. Lay compliance cannot be dismissed in terms of submission to ecclesiastical authority—armed as it was with the coercive power of the canon law, extending over the whole range of what we now call the enforcement of morals—or of a craven fear of the devils in hell. None of these suffices to explain the lavish architecture and furnishing, for instance, of late mediaeval churches—their naves, aisles and towers (which were a lay responsibility) generally more elaborate than their chancels (the clerical responsibility)—nor the multiplication of lay books of devotion which spread with the newly distributed wealth of the fifteenth century.

The later Middle Ages saw the growth of a genuine lay mysticism and spirituality, evidenced in England in Walter Hilton, Richard Rolle, Julian of Norwich, and even in funny old Margery Kempe. In Europe it produced the more formal literature and structures of the *Devotio Moderna*. The growth was spontaneous, yet the material of growth was the traditional material: a contemplation of the events of the life of Jesus and the hopes which it occasioned. And it created its own social expressions, some in new communities and associations, some in movements of protest against the established social order.

Its product in terms of personality is harder to assess. Evidence for it could be sought in the secular literature of the period, for example in *Piers Plowman*, *The Paston Letters*, *The Shillingford Correspondence* and the like. Professor Du Boulay[4] suggests that there was a clear moral or conscientious advance in the late fourteenth and the fifteenth centuries in England, on the evidence of this literature, and this despite the inevitably dulling effects of formalism and the obligation of secular persuasions to conform with some religious observances which had lost their inherent spiritual or moral force. One significant product of the 'system' was those minds, for example of Erasmus, More, Colet and Christopher St German, able and sensitive enough to criticize it, all of whom saw in it the possibility of a genuine and effective reformation not the inevitability of its destruction.

The Reformation brought, in some sense, mere loss. It took the warmth out of moral persuasions by destroying the intimate fellowship of the Virgin Mother and the saints. It substituted moralistic, minatory preaching, based more on the denunciations of the Old Testament prophets than on the hope and joys of the heavenly city and its denizens. It led into a Puritanism in linear succession to mediaeval 'Catholic' Puritanism, but more dangerous. The Catholic tradition had contained Puritanism by embodying it primarily in certain communities vowed to the way of renunciation, co-existing with the way of affirmation, triumph and glory in the Church at large. Protestant Puritanism universalized it, tried to impose it on everybody, with civil and social sanctions even more pervasive—and more quickly repudiated—than the old canonical ones. Mercifully the old tradition of reason survived this and asserted itself again in the greater divines, Anglican and Reformed—Richard Hooker,* Bishop Sanderson, Richard Baxter and Jeremy Taylor.[8] Significant for our purpose are the titles of Taylor's treatises, *The Rule and Exercises of Holy Living* and *The Rule and Exercises of Holy Dying*: 'rule' implies something *given*: 'exercises' implies something to be done by oneself. The age of toleration, too, had dawned.

With William Law a new mysticism came in, softening the asperities of both moralism and reason with a pervasive inner light—borrowed, indeed, from a mystical tradition on the Continent which had carried over from the *Devotio Moderna* of later Catholicism. Law's moral appeal is manifestly to an inner spirit and motivation, supported indeed by social expectation but not reliant upon enforcement. This is even more evident in his *Spirit of Love* than in his *A Serious Call to a Devout and Holy Life*.

The Counter-Reformation intensified two elements from the mediaeval tradition: devotion to the person of Christ and the 'saving mysteries', which it systematized to a degree unknown before; and personal discipline of mind and imagination as well as of body. But there was this difference: it was a personal, individualistic endeavour, in substitution for the corporate, social discipline of the mediaeval community, which had ceased to be. Scupoli's *Spiritual Combat* was one of the many manuals of this sort of discipline with which the Counter-Reformation and the printing presses together covered the prayer-desks of Europe. These manuals, translated into English during the Catholic revival in nineteenth-century England, restored this strong, individualistic type

---

* Hooker's words on education match the group's discussion of the subject: "Education and instruction are the means, the one by use, the other by precept, to make our natural faculty of reason both the better and the sooner able to judge rightly between truth and error, good and evil. But at what time a man may be said to have attained so far forth the use of reason, as sufficeth to make him capable of those Laws, whereby he is then bound to guide his actions; this is a great deal more easy for common sense to discern, than for any man by skill and learning to determine; even as it is not in philosophers, who best know the nature both of fire and of gold, to teach what degree of the one will serve to purify the other, so well as the artisan who doth this by fire discerneth by sense when the fire hath that degree of heat which sufficeth for his purpose."[7]

of personal discipline into English Christian teaching at a time when character building became, with Thomas Arnold and his successors, a major preoccupation of the English public school system. This was able to clothe itself, as often as not, in the language of a newly vigorous and authoritarian Evangelical Christianity, which set before its adherents the twin aims of benevolence and evangelism towards others, and the pursuit of holiness in their own persons. At the same time, in society at large, the seeds were being sown of that fundamental doubt about *all* authorities, not in religion only but also in philosophy, politics, conventions, child care and education, which were to flower in the twentieth century to great effect.

Doubtless there are many significant errors and omissions in the broad sweep across the tradition which has been the subject of this paper. After all allowance for these has been made, however, the conclusion is inescapable that, in the Christian tradition, in all that we now term 'the development of personality' there has been, throughout, a strong and ineradicable element, not only authoritative in content but also authoritarian in its manner of presentation. It was grounded on a certain confidence about the end of man—a relationship of some sort with God; about what God has done to make this attainable; and about what God required if it were to be attained.

Inevitably, therefore, the initial Christian reaction was predictably hostile to the insights into human character and motivation associated with Freud, and the prescriptions for conduct derived from them. Psychology and psychiatry, in their early years, encountered much misunderstanding which would have been less likely had their practitioners invented a specific and technical language of their own (as the old physicians had done) rather than use words already current and laden with meanings and overtones of their own. 'Guilt', for example, is a word over which subsequent misunderstanding was inevitable. Sexuality, also inevitably, became a shuttlecock in the battle; and, battered and broken though the feathers are, it is still in play across the court because neither side is entirely sure how to knock it out. In the old tradition the erotic imagination was held to be dangerous in itself. In so far as it gave ground first to marital and then to parental love, it was licit; but it was always dangerous, and to be checked.

This tradition is a whole world away from the new mind which not only affirms the lawfulness of sexual pleasure in itself—and searches for more sophisticated and infallible contraception in its service—but exalts also the erotic imagination, using every cultural art to excite it. I do not judge or condemn this situation. I say that we are bewildered by it. It is symptomatic of our confusion about what the process of growth in personality both is and demands: and particularly about the relative degrees of freedom and authority properly required by the process.*

It may be that at any point in my survey the notion of 'freedom' might be read-in where I have written 'authority'. But if, on balance, my interpretation is broadly right by the narrowest of margins, it would follow that our task now is not to try to re-interpret the tradition in pursuit of a freedom or openness which we vainly wish were there, but to recognize the fact that we have now to reckon with a new concept, a new approach to personality and its growth not met with before, measure its worth in its own terms and deal with it accordingly. The enterprise which the Personality and Science group undertook was precisely to explore the ingredients of personality as understood in the relevant scientific disciplines, and to see what understanding of man and, perhaps, what prescriptions for man, could be grounded upon these ingredients.

What reflections relevant to this paper arise from the deliberations of the group? There has emerged from a review of the empirically discerned ingredients of 'personality' a plastic or malleable view highly congenial to the Christian theologian (p. 125). Personality, we have learned, is a matrix, a cluster of forces and activities recognizable or given discernible form by two characteristics. The first is a capacity for freedom, for self-determination; the second is a capacity for social interaction, for mutuality; and this second is shown partly by a capacity for making recognizably 'human' gestures, and partly by a capacity for awakening recognizably 'human' responses. The second part of the second characteristic is important, although overlooked more often in discussion than in practice. A decerebrate patient, for instance, may have lost the capacity for any self-determination and for making human gestures; but while he lives and breathes spontaneously he is still to those about him a 'he' and not an 'it'. He awakens from them human responses, so that they tend, wash, feed him and so on; and they themselves exhibit 'humanity', at the very least, in doing so. In short, the aspect of mutuality, of interdependence, which in infancy manifests itself before the capacity for self-determination is developed, can also survive it at the other end of the life-span, and perhaps show itself to be the more enduring of the two aspects and the more significant for philosophy, theology and ethics. It is out of the relationships of the infant with those about him that the capacity for self-determination will arise, or be prevented from arising if those relationships be unfavourable. Relationship, mutuality, is prior to freedom.

This is precisely the theological point underlying the Christian approach to human personality. Christian theology begins with relation-

---

* Some penetrating theological explorations of the new attitude to sexuality are to be found in *Esprit*, n.s. 11 (Nov., 1960), in *Lumière et Vie*, 97 (March-May, 1970), and, more summarily, in *"The Humanization of Sexuality"*, *Concilium*, v, 6 (May, 1970).

ship—that initiated by God, witnessed to by Hebrew prophets, psalmists and law-givers, made evident and humanly understandable in Jesus Christ, and offered to all men through the agency of the Church. What the Church has called its 'gospel' is the ground of the relationship into which it invites those who hear. In proclaiming that gospel the Church is necessarily authoritative, because it believes it has something 'given'—however disclosed—to say and cannot without apostasy refrain from saying it. The *response* to this proclamation must necessarily be free—it cannot be enforced. Where the gospel is so presented that freedom is impugned, where, for instance, appeals are made improperly to the emotions or to fear, or where social, political, penal or economic pressures or inducements impair the integrity of the response, then the gospel itself is betrayed (because of the violence done to its central affirmations) and the whole concept of relationship is distorted; growth, if it begins at all, begins upon a wrong footing and along a wrong course. But once the proper response has been made, 'freedom' is to some extent *ipso facto* limited: the respondent henceforth moves no longer in a world of infinite possibilities; his mind, intentions, personality are, by his own decision, directed towards an End, with its related dependent, intermediate ends, which by definition exclude others. Again, throughout his journey towards that End each related end is, in the last analysis, something to be freely chosen, but there is a logical sense in which the choice could not be free. Granted the End, and the position reached in the journey towards it and the circumstances given on any particular occasion of choice, *this* choice might be the only one open. To choose another course might be to choose the wrong one, from which a return might be required by means of other choices towards the End. Freedom is somehow circumscribed by 'authority'—the authority of the reality disclosed in the gospel about the nature (and therefore the will) of the God who is the End.

The plasticity of man in relationship has another interest for the Christian theologian, for he teaches that Christian character is moulded, or developed, precisely in relationship, not only with human society in all its manifestations but also with God immanent, or indwelling, through one whom theology has called a 'Person'—the Holy Spirit. The word *character* is itself symbolic. It is derived from the Greek word for a graving tool, that which would cut a cameo or engrave a seal; and so it is transferred to the mark, image or impression made, for example, by the typographer's letter upon the page or by the seal upon wax. Now Christian theology, since St Paul, has described what we now call the development of personality precisely in these terms. The goal of Christian living, in terms limited for this discussion, is to acquire the mark or stamp, the seal or character or image of Christ—the *impress* of him as a living person upon the plastic wax of personality. The achieving of this is a work of a relationship in which there is a continuity of free responses, as delineated above, to something, someone, authoritatively given. The Church's function is continually to disclose both it and him in such a fashion that the response is invited and becomes possible. The Church is at liberty—and under obligation—to vary its method, its idiom and presentation, from generation to generation. It is not at liberty to vary the 'given', though it is continuously under duty to discover for itself, in every age, precisely what this 'given' is and to realize it, make it real in its own experience and presentation.

These are general reflections upon a general obligation. The obligation accepted, particular questions may be examined subject to it. The theologian, when examining all the procedures by which personality may be changed, will wish to inquire, as strictly as any other specialist, into the nature and effect of those changes on all the empirical features of the life of the person involved, be he patient or prisoner. He may be bound to ask, *qua* theologian, further questions which the other specialists involved, in relation to their proper disciplines, need not ask (questions concerning the development of this personality in its relationship with God, its restoration into the image of God discernible in the image or mark of Christ). The theologian ought to ask those questions; the other specialists may have to ask them also. If, for instance, a psychiatrist understands that his patient accepts for himself something like the Christian vocation and obligation described in this paper, and if that psychiatrist truly respects the personality of his patient and his liberty to entertain such a vocation and obligation, then the psychiatrist cannot but take account of this element in his professional treatment of the patient. Such a consideration would seem to lie behind the request which is often voiced for 'a Christian psychiatrist' and which some psychiatrists are known to respect, whether they themselves profess Christian belief or not.

Full treatment of this theme lies beyond the range of this paper but the direction in which this fuller treatment might go may be seen from an examination of a few of the instances chosen for scientific exploration in this book. Castration for offenders convicted of sexual or other forms of aggression is one example (p. 25). The arguments advanced in favour of the operation avoid the cruder opposition of the interests of the individual to the interests of society. They claim a benefit for the individual and for society: the individual is delivered from a long term of imprisonment and from the constant fear of committing another offence; society is delivered from the risk of his aggression and from the expense of keeping him in unprofitable custody for many years. These benefits are gained, it is admitted, at the cost of the individual's loss of what is generally accounted to be a fundamental natural endowment—his virility. Into this word are compacted two elements, the right to that full expression of masculinity which, in general, makes possible a full range of human relationships in a bisexual humanity, and the right to procreation. The theologian's first task (after joining with his scientific colleagues in requiring the fullest possible follow-up studies of persons so castrated and returned to life in society) is to elucidate such statements about natural endowments and natural rights and to examine their relevance to the case.

Historically it is probable that the procreative aspect of virility has meant more than the relational. Throughout human history, until the recent past, the earth remained to be subdued, the forests cut back, the soil cultivated, the seas and rivers fished, and enemies, both animals and men, to be fought. For this, man had to populate the earth; with high mortality, population growth was slow. Fertility was valued. Religion, too, demanded children, male children, for they it was, at least in the Hebrew culture, who carried the name; in them a man lived on after his death, his only hope of immortality. Other cultures gave children other sacred functions, in the name of religion. In all cultures men grow old and require children to support and protect them in old age. The capacity to procreate, therefore, was essential for survival, individual and corporate, and presumably for these practical reasons it became invested with the language of a 'natural right', meeting a natural necessity.

If this right is to be defended now, the defence must rest on other grounds. On a world scale (though not uniformly in every region) survival requires a restriction not an acceleration of population growth. In Christian cultures the hope of life after death stands on another ground—the resurrection of Jesus Christ from the dead—and in secularized Western cultures, where this belief drove out the earlier beliefs before it was itself discarded, there is no express hope of surviving death at all. In advanced technological societies economic support of the aged becomes a charge on the corporate wealth, whether through insurance or pensions or provisions of social security; emotional support may be lacking but even this could in theory be supplied by community action. If, therefore, the old 'natural right' to a capacity for procreation stood on these demographic, economic and religious grounds, it requires a new justification as these grounds cease to support it.

On the relational aspect, the Western Hebrew-Christian tradition has been ambivalent. The older of the Creation myths in Genesis (2, 4–24) says plainly that woman was given to man to be a help meet for him, that is, to be in a relation with him which nothing else yet created could supply; the procreative aspect appeared in the later, more stylized version now in Genesis 1. In the early centuries of the Christian era the relational aspect lost value, though not without theological protest.[1] The new asceticism, intensified from non-Christian sources, taught the

117

necessity to deliver oneself if possible from sexual desire, though the Council of Nicaea voiced the consistent and formal judgment of the Church when, in the year 325, it authoritatively forbade castration as the means.[3] The proper means were those generally prescribed for the Christian life, the exercise of the will enabled by grace. The sexual complementarity of marriage was grudgingly conceded in this tradition as incidental to the rearing of children. The higher way was that of renunciation, preferably under a vow of chastity in a religious community, whether of monks or of nuns. It was not difficult later, therefore, to condone the employment of *castrati* in the Italian and papal choirs, despite the condemnations of earlier Councils and Fathers and despite the theological abhorrence of the Hebrew tradition which excluded eunuchs from the Covenant.* While, therefore, in theory the Western tradition would defend the natural right to marry and attach to it the natural obligation to rear children, in practice the right was much restricted. Serfs enjoyed no such right at all—the word *contubernium* (the concubinage of slaves) was still applied to their unions in the language of ecclesiastical administration in the mid-fifteenth century, and their issue was called their *sequela*.[8] The marriages of the free were disposable for dynastic, territorial or commercial advantage; children could be given in tender years to the cloister, from which it might be easier in theory than in practice to escape without a life profession. When slave-owning in the plantations of the New World replaced serfdom on the manors of the Old, the same denial of the right to marry carried over. The language of natural rights, therefore, begins to lack substance when we begin to examine it in relation to how the sexual endowment of man has been treated in the history of the West.

What has been achieved in very recent times, and entrenched in the laws of civilized society, is a right to protection against any physical impairment of sexual capacity *without consent*. (This is different from speaking of a right to consent to such an impairment. English common law, for instance, does not recognize consent to any mutilation unless the mutilation can be justified on the ground of necessity—that is, the operation, for example the amputation of a part of the body, is necessary for the good of the whole body and that no less drastic means are eligible to achieve that end.) This advance in the recognition of liberty over authority sharpened the severity of the moral judgment passed on the enforced sterilization of Jews and other victims of the Nazi tyranny. The Nuremberg Code of 1947 and the Declaration of Helsinki of 1964 (the code of ethics of the World Medical Association on human experimentation) represent attempts to assure by convention that such evils shall not be practised again. But what *is* 'consent' in the context of a penal institution for criminal psychopaths, or even less dangerous sexual

---

* Deuteronomy 23, 1; Isaiah 56, 3–5; Acts 8, 27–29

offenders, from which release or parole may be obtained upon condition of castration? This is the heart of the question.

The Nuremberg Code on permissible medical experiments treats the question of consent at length in its first clause:

"1. The voluntary consent of the human subject is absolutely essential. This means that the person involved should have legal capacity to give consent; should be so situated as to be able to exercise free power of choice, without the intervention of any element of force, fraud, deceit, duress, overreaching, or other ulterior form of constraint or coercion; and should have sufficient knowledge and comprehension of the elements of the subject matter involved as to enable him to make an understanding and enlightened decision . . . ."

These are stringent conditions, and, no doubt, in a civilized country like Denmark every formal provision is made to see that they are met. Castration is not penally imposed; the offender/patient must himself seek permission from the Ministry of Justice for the operation, and his application must be backed by a medical recommendation given only after a thorough examination of the man and a discussion with him of the issues involved. But inevitably the man is subject to circumstantial pressure—that of the urge for release from detention, that of the fear of committing a further offence with all its consequences—and so inevitably the real decision lies with the physician in charge of him, whose power over him derives not only from the custodial relationship but also from the superiority of knowledge. He has authority over an inevitably divided and unfree man, whose freedom was, perhaps, congenitally restricted by his endocrine endowment and then further impaired, socially and psychologically, by whatever acts constituted his criminal offence.

The physician's responsibility, therefore, is great, if only to maximize the freedom of the man's consent. His problem is more difficult because of the poverty of adequate follow-up studies of the effect of castration upon personality and relationships, social and (the theologian would add) religious. In earlier cultures, Jewish and Christian, religion has merely reflected the social ambiguities: the eunuch was useful, in the court, the harem, the choir; but his condition was termed 'unnatural'; as a man he was incomplete, second class. 'Unnatural', in this context, ceases to be a descriptive word; it becomes morally loaded, because of the general moral approbation given to heterosexual capacities and relationships, which alone are accounted 'natural'. A society which has only recently begun to try to free itself from this ingrained habit of judgment is still a potentially hostile environment into which to launch the newly castrated. So the cost has to be counted: to the man, and to his family, if he is surgically impaired, to society if he is not.

Hope turns to a better way of achieving the same end. Probably surgical castration is obsolescent. A chemical method of controlling the endocrine balance might reduce the man's potential for harm and so also the ground of fear in himself and in society. The administration of drugs would be controlled: it could be varied or discontinued according to need and presumably the finality of castration would be absent. This sounds more promising, especially in the wider flexibility it would give to consent. But it must be observed that authority will still maintain its hold over personality. The patient will be utterly dependent, for the preservation of his hormonal balance, and therefore of his social stability and (so far as all succeeds) for his freedom from encounter with the law, upon those clinically in charge of him. How far a clinician has a responsibility to society which may influence his responsibility to his patient is now one of the debatable points of medical ethics. And if the clinical relationship has been initiated by order of a court, after conviction for an offence, the protection of society *is* a relevant factor in the treatment of the patient, as also is the effect of the treatment upon his personality.

Considerations of a similar sort would attend the question of the enforcement of medical treatment upon a non-criminal medical risk. Should there be statutory power to enforce immunization upon a known typhoid carrier? Or if the link between the XYY chromosome and psychopathology became so precisely established that it was possible to predict that a particular person, given a certain environment, would commit a serious act of aggression, perhaps murder, within a predictable time, would it be right forcibly to remove him from that environment, perhaps into custody, or to enforce upon him an appropriate treatment (if one were known) calculated to reduce the risk? Ideally, one would work for consent. But that might not be given. What then? The abortion of a foetus in which there is a statistical probability of congenital deformity is a variant of the same type of case. At present this requires the consent of the mother; but it is possible to envisage a so rapidly mounting pressure of public opinion that that consent becomes proportionately less free; and the logical end of that process, if we were to reach it, might be routine or even enforced termination for specified foetal risks, including the XYY chromosome detected antenatally.

These contemporary illustrations are related to the more general study with which this paper began because of their bearing on the question of authority and freedom in relation to personal life and personality. To the modern freedom-conscious mind, with its proper respect for all that we mean by self-determination, the old authorities of religion are suspect. Men are glad to be freed, on the whole, from an authority which thought it better that they should be pressed into heaven than that they should not attain it at all. But for centuries men accepted that authority and that pressure (while kicking as men will against them) because, in their fundamental assumptions about life, they accepted the end towards which these were the means. Man is in no very different position today in relation to the vastly greater power of medical science. If, in our group mentality, our fundamental corporate assumptions, we accept certain ends, we submit thereby to unimagined pressures and authorities as the means. If the ends are personal, like the prolongation of life, we submit to deeply penetrating assaults, surgical, pharmacological or psychiatric, upon our persons, committing ourselves totally into the hands of men, specialists of sorts, as the necessary means. If the ends are social, we accept one invasion of our individuality, or our psycho-physical and social freedom, after another; we debate the threats which we detect while more consolidate themselves undetected; and even those which we debate take hold in the end. We are still free enough at least to discuss our freedom, but not so free that we can look with detachment upon the shackles of authority in the past. It is in relation to the ends that we pursue that we debate the ethics of our means.

SUMMARY

Since 'Personality and Science' has not been considered as such in the theological tradition, which has had other aims and interests, some translation is necessary for the working-out of a sequence of relevant reflections. The theological concern presupposed a set of relationships, particularly that of the person with God, and would not isolate the development of personality from this context.

In the Hebrew-Christian tradition there have been two major relevant assertions. The first embodies a doctrine of God and man so advanced as to exert its own authoritative claim. The second demands a response to this claim of such a sort that man can thereby attain that freedom and self-determination which are proper to his nature; but, such is his relational nature, his freedom is achieved not by repudiation of authority but in response to it, properly conceived: *cui servire est regnare*.

In the final section the question of authority and personality is examined with reference to castration and other medical procedures discussed elsewhere in this book.

REFERENCES

1. ASHBY, G. W. (1969). *Theology* **72**, 482.

2. BROWN, P. (1967). *Augustine of Hippo*. London: Faber.

3. CHURCH ASSEMBLY BOARD FOR SOCIAL RESPONSIBILITY (1962). In *Sterilization: an Ethical Enquiry*, p. 17 and app. C. London: Church Information Office.

4. DU BOULAY, F. R. H. (1970). *An Age of Ambition*. London: Nelson.

5. DUNSTAN, G. R. (ed.) (1963, 1967). *The Register of Edmund Lacy, Bishop of Exeter, 1420–1455*, **1**, p. 59; **3**, pp. 217, 220. London: Canterbury and York Society.

6. GALLAY, J. (1955). *Rech. Sci. religieuse* **43**, 545.

7. HOOKER, R. (1594). In *The Laws of Ecclesiastical Policy* **1**, vi, 5.

8. TAYLOR, J. (1650, 1651). *The Rule and Exercises of Holy Living*; and *The Rule and Exercises of Holy Dying*.

DISCUSSION

In this section a picture of an authoritarian structure of personality with both genuine and distorted features was developed. In the nineteenth century it was taken for granted that self-control was an important virtue. At that time a man would have a definite sense of values. He would be aware of an intention to achieve something, using his talents and skills as the raw materials on which to work. He would relax and enjoy himself only in so far as was compatible with this overall purpose. He called this way of life authoritarian as presupposing a determinative hierarchy of values in accordance with which a man should steer his life and not drift. The corruption of this concept become known as the fag end of the Protestant ethic, which expressed the view that the object of life is success, man justifies himself by competing with others and asceticism is built-in only as a necessity to this end. The present revolt against the authoritarian personality was more against this corrupt form than against the genuine one. In the Christian tradition a certain sort of authoritarian structure of personality is unavoidable. Skills and talents are a gift from God, to be used in his service and in the service of man, and therefore the individual must be self-determining; he cannot entirely relax and enjoy life irrespective of purpose. This self-determining personality is not only an end in itself but a contribution to a wider whole. Doubt was expressed about whether this was the proper usage for the word authoritarian, which is probably related more to the compelling of one man by another than to a man who decides purposefully for himself. There is a distinction between the authority of God mediated (*a*) in relationships (which would be authoritative and not authoritarian), and (*b*) through a fixed text or infallible doctrine, which would be highly authoritarian. People could respond freely to authority but not to authoritarianism. Freedom is found in some kind of response matching something authoritatively given. The psychological equivalent of authority communicated in relationships might be called emotional insight. Authoritarian would denote one will (say, the psychiatrist's) imposing itself over another (the patient's). Understanding should be something to be exploited in a good sense, not imposed.

The fierce authoritarianism of St Paul and St Augustine, especially of the latter about sex, was noted. Paul's profound understanding of grace (a relationship with God) and freedom, combined with his apparent

122

necessity to establish his own authority against St Peter and the other Apostles, may have encouraged his authoritarian behaviour and writing. Similarly, Augustine's guilt about his early sex life may have had the same effect. Some aggressive aspects of sexual drives today need new outlets because other routes (for example, war) are now restricted. Religion, like art, seems, temporarily at any rate, to fail to offer alternative outlets.

14: Human Personality

I. T. RAMSEY

LOOKING back over earlier papers in which we have discussed various developments in science and medicine, we may now ask ourselves what views about human personality do these discussions presuppose or imply. Human personality and the changes that scientific and medical knowledge and skills can bring about or expect to bring about have been discussed in the context of leucotomy, drugs, psychology and psychiatry, and endocrinology. The relevant question which now arises is this. How do all these understandings of human personality fit together? To what view of human personality do they point? With what wider views of personality may they be consistent?

The first answer, which scarcely goes beyond a summary of the facts, would be that human personality consists of a complex matrix of many interacting factors—psychological, biochemical, endocrine (inborn and acquired) and no doubt many unknown. This account concentrates the answer in a single concept—matrix—pointing to some kind of unity. One reason why the word matrix can be used in this way, as a pointer to some kind of unity, is that these various factors do interact and for that very reason suggest some kind of embracing, unifying function for the mutually related variables. For instance, in any illness, but especially in psychosomatic illness, a vicious circle may arise between factors called respectively 'functional' and 'organic'. The organic factors can be internal (endocrine, biochemical, physiological) or external (for example drugs or even foodstuffs), and the functional factors will be psychological and sociological. Abnormalities in any of these may start an illness but by the time a patient seeks professional help both kinds of factor are usually active. Hence, either organic or psychological treatment can be partially effective in psychosomatic illness. The example of anorexia nervosa has already been mentioned (pp. 22, 23). This combination of factors points to cross-referencing between them and also supports the idea that personality is normally, and in some kind of way, a mutually balancing unity.

At the same time, we must not suppose too simple an interrelationship, too stereotyped a unity nor, especially, that personality is entirely a matter of brain structure. We must not suppose, for example, that the unity of personality could be entirely accounted for in cerebral terms and that mental illness is wholly reducible to structural changes within the brain, and is therefore basically similar to a bodily disease. As

125

Dr Thomas Freeman remarked (p. 54) "For some [psychiatrists] mental illness is the result of physical disease; for others, it is the expression of an inability to adapt to the demands of life." And Freud (see p. 54) eventually concluded that most mental events cannot be satisfactorily explained in terms of brain dysfunction.

So, whatever more might need saying about personality being a complex matrix, it seems clear that to analyse this concept wholly in terms of brain structure will be inadequate. But brain structure may be a useful model or picture by which to point at, represent or symbolize what is meant by speaking of someone's personality, or of personality as a unity.

The observation that biochemical and/or endocrine factors have no clear-cut, stereotyped effect on psychosomatic illness underlines the fact that personality is no simple function of such factors, and may well be thought to suggest that there is in personality some kind of relatively stable centre or control. It seems, for example, that hormones can only act on a *basic* personality matrix already present.

A distinction between 'character' and 'temperament' may be very illuminating here. If we define temperament as being related to a person's moods (what some might call his personality traits) then we might say that temperament is connected with hormonal effects. Character, however, would relate to a person's ability to organize or control his life in some ordered way, an order which would exhibit implicitly or explicitly principles or rules. So, for example, if a given endocrine abnormality gave rise to increased aggression, a strong character while feeling more agressive would be able to control the aggression, whereas a weak character might be overwhelmed by the feeling of aggressiveness which ultimately might induce madness. It seems, therefore, that here again personality or character relates to some kind of inner control or unifying centre. It will be clear that such reflections as these lead easily to a 'citadel' model or picture of personality (p. 93). But even Professor Hare's appeal to a man's interests (p. 97) would have to be broad enough to embrace a set of ideals and values and these, in organizing and deciding preferences between various possibilities, introduce again the idea of a unity. Indeed, I do not believe that Professor Hare would take exception to a phrase used by Professor Mitchell who speaks of persons as "self-directing and with a clear sense of values." (p. 101). Such a view of a person as self-directing surely points to human personality as some kind of unity.

These reflections could be linked with a psychological approach to personality in which strength of personality or personal health might be defined in terms of adaptability in meeting external stresses, that is, the ability to come to terms with a whole variety of outside buffets. Personality defined in this way would relate to a capacity to meet actively and thus to overcome external forces.

126

This context broadens to give a wider background to points which arose when we discussed drugs, leucotomy and penal medicine. One presupposition of that discussion was that a person should have the maximum possible contact with, and control over, the circumstances in which he finds himself. This indeed is one understanding of freedom. Hence, drug *addiction* is judged to be bad because in this case human personality is oppressed and conquered. For the same kind of reason, some would be against the enforcement of treatment (for example castration for repeated sexual offences) as a condition of release from prison. Again, it might be said that a leucotomy raises the wider issues it does, precisely because it imposes restrictions on a person's control over his environment insofar as certain possible reactions and attitudes are now excluded. Once again personality is being interpreted in terms of effective activity. The same analysis of personality in terms of active control no doubt lies behind protests against legal persecutions for the 'mere possession' of drugs. Further, the adolescent who rebels against parental authority or who responds in a certain way to deprivation is acting in principle like an addict who seeks freedom, ironically, by taking drugs. All are endeavours after self-realization, self-fulfilment and self-understanding; all are endeavours to exercise an outgoing, self-expression activity. Some might even say that this was an expression of the aggression which characterizes all human nature and which reaches abnormal and irrational proportions in the attitude and activities of so-called hell's angels and skinheads. Conversely, the flower people were finding self-realization in protesting against the institutionalized violence of society.

But personality is no isolated control centre of activity; it only exists in a social context or environment. It is significant that many addicts seem to need to belong to a group and find their drug addiction all the more attractive when they can 'take a trip' with others. So there emerges the view that a particular personality is one centre of activity—an 'owned' activity—in a cluster of activities forming some specific social group.

This same view of personality is also presupposed by an attitude to life and death, especially death, implicit in many medical judgments. A particular treatment would normally be condemned if it decreased life expectancy. The longer a life the better. And not only is a high mortality rate deemed to be bad but death itself is looked upon as a clinical failure. What emerges from these judgments is a view of death as the cessation of all social activity.

All this suggests that the one unifying concept, definitive of personality, is not soul nor mind nor body. There is no kind of underlying cushion to which all our bodily and mental events and characteristics are attached as pins; and any basic personality matrix is not static. Rather is personality to be analysed in terms of a distinctive activity, distinctive in being owned, localized, personalized. The unity of personality on this view is to be found in an integrating activity, an activity expressed, embodied and scientifically understood in terms of its genetic, bio-chemical and endocrine, electronic, neurological and psychological manifestations. What we call human behaviour is an expression of that effective, integrating activity which is peculiarly and distinctively ourselves.

In this way our discussions have also pointed us to a goal which is not normality but increasingly effective activity within a social group.

How does a Christian conceptual framework house these presup-positions? How well do these views thrown up by our scientific dis-cussion harmonize with Christian ideas of personality and human nature? To answer the question let us ask what is the Christian view of persons. The short answer is that a Christian view of personality arises as an understanding of what a man is when he responds to a disclosure of God in Christ; when he responds actively to what inspires him about the love and grace of God in Jesus Christ; and when in so responding he finds himself a member of that community which is the Christian Church. There is therefore no disparity between the Christian view of personality and that which has been presupposed by the bio-medical discussions summarized above.

Let me now endeavour to set out this view at somewhat greater length. To the question: 'What is man?' the obvious answer is: 'A combined topic of the natural and behavioural sciences.' Biophysics, biochemistry, molecular biology, anatomy, pathology, endocrinology, neurology, psychology, social studies, economics—all these and many other disciplines will tell us, as we have seen, a great deal about man. Further, there is virtually no limit to the number of such scientific disciplines and no limit to the range of any one of them. To what they have to say about man can be added what each of us introspects and recognizes as our dream images, memory images and so on. Again, as our discussions have shown and other papers make clear, human behaviour can be influenced in far-reaching ways by drugs, leucotomy and hormones. The disciplined and reliable can be changed into the careless and casual. What more, then, needs to be said? Is man no more than the combined topic of the natural and behavioural sciences? Is his behaviour ade-quately understood as a subject for increasing frontier work between several sciences? Do socially responsible citizens differ significantly from house-trained dogs?

Let us argue by a *reductio ad absurdum*. Suppose nothing more were to be said about human beings. Then each human being would be a set—admittedly very complex—of discriminated observables, scientific objects, discerned behaviour patterns, a set of these and no more.

This may seem not at all implausible about everybody—except ourselves. As an account by ourselves of ourselves it would clearly be a logical blunder. For any of us to talk of a group of *objects* presupposes a correlative *subject*. Whatever is observed implies an observer who is a presupposition of the resultant discourse and cannot be netted within it. The trouble is that third-person assertions always look so ultimate, reliable and complete whether it be 'blue copper sulphate turns white on heating' or 'the penny is brown'. Yet in fact all such assertions are within invisible quotes, so that a logically complete assertion is always in the first person. The invisible quotes are in fact deliberately erased when the assertion has gained, or in principle could gain, sufficient individual support as to make it useful general currency within society at large, useful for purposes which need take no account of the personal framework in which it was set, and wish indeed to disregard such sub-jective attachments. But while being in that sense reliable in a trans-personal sense, these assertions are unreliable if taken to be adequate about all that there is, and about persons in particular. For the price they have paid for their peculiar reliability is to be in principle unreliable as accounts of what is distinctive about human beings. Further, there is no question of this 'I'—which indicates the active observer—being progressively eroded as scientific disciplines develop, for he is, as I have tried to show, a presupposition of all scientific discourse from first to last no matter how little or how far that discourse has developed.

So far I have been concerned to give a logical argument in favour of a transcendent 'I'—transcendent in the sense that it is not to be contained within scientific discourse nor reduced to terms within such discourse. But the question now arises: What in fact is this to which 'I' distinctively refers and about which first-person assertions distinctively talk? How do we gain access to this which makes us distinctively ourselves, dis-tinctively human beings?

Plainly, not by observation. For, as David Hume clearly showed, that would be to produce not subjectivity but just another set of observ-ables. We only gain access to ourselves, we only know that about which first-person assertions distinctively talk, by self-disclosure. We become aware of our transcendent subjectivity as and when each of us comes to himself, comes alive, affirms himself in a disclosure situation; and this only occurs when a story about observables takes on depth, reveals another dimension. It is significant that we can only point to what we are speaking of by using metaphorical phrases—models such as these. When a disclosure situation occurs we do not find our subjectivity laid before us as an object; rather we realize and affirm our subjectivity in making our subjective response, in subjectively coming alive correla-tively with some objective disclosure, that is, with what has come alive objectively.

129

As an example of a story told with this intention of self-disclosure, a story designed to reveal subjectivity, who and what a person really is, we may take the parable which Nathan told David in II Samuel 12. David, not content with his many wives, had cast covetous glances at his neighbour's wife, Bath-sheba, and had contrived to get her husband killed in battle so that the complications of an involved situation could be conveniently resolved with least embarrassment to himself. Along comes Nathan and tells a story of two men—one rich, the other poor. One has many flocks and herds, the other a little ewe lamb. When the rich man had to provide for an unexpected dinner party with friends, rather than take one of his own flock he took the ewe lamb which meant everything to the family who owned it. David, as the judge, was profoundly moved—"The man that hath done this shall surely die and he shall restore the lamb fourfold." Here was an objective reading of the situation. It might look like a moral judgment, but it was more like a legal judgment with overtones of emotion. There had certainly been no self-disclosure. To effect this, Nathan drew out the isomorphism between the story of the ewe lamb and the action of David. A pattern was repeated in the two empiric incidents and the link phrase was "Thou art the man . . .". The light dawned, the encounter with Nathan took on depth, another dimension. David had come to himself, realized his subjectivity, realized himself as a man and as a moral agent.

The story illustrates the general point that we are characteristically ourselves when we acknowledge and respond to the authority of a moral claim, to the vision of a moral obligation. In this context the specifically Christian answer to the question 'What is man?' and 'What may man be?' will be given when those who ask the question respond to the disclosure of God in Christ, to that activity of God of which they are aware when a story centred around the historic events of Christ's life and ministry takes on depth, another dimension, comes alive to inspire. Putting the point in a little more detail, there is for St Paul, at least in theory, the natural man, the man who is nothing but a combined topic of the natural and behavioural sciences, who receiveth not the things of the Spirit of God (I Corinthians 2, 14), whose life is restricted to the natural world; the man who in one sense does not live as distinct from existing. But there is by contrast the 'spiritual man' who discerns the things of the Spirit of God, who (we may alternatively translate) is braced by the wind of God blowing in his face, who realizes himself as he responds to the activity of God disclosed in Christ, who 'sees' the deep things of God, the activities of God known in a situation of depth. Here is the spiritual man, defined by a specific kind of activity—the basic personality matrix which he realizes as he responds to the gospel— who finds his life and freedom in responding to what he discerns in depth. Here is the man who in theological terms is saved and made whole and who, under the inspiration of the haunting vision of the gospel, can pioneer whatever changes come to man or society as scientific exploration takes us further into unknown and exciting terrain. He goes forward in faith, confident that under the inspiration of his vision there can be a creative outcome to the travail in which we endeavour to match medico-scientific developments with the needs and possibilities of human life and society.

Here, then, in a personality which each of us discovers in an active self-response to a disclosure of God's activity in Christ, is for the Christian that which unifies, that which is distinctive of each of us. This is that to which the word 'soul' was meant to point; that which can be expressed in directed thought or bodily activity. Here is no metaphysical substructure or pin-cushion, no static centre, but that which we know in being active, in realizing ourselves. Here is the permanent complement of all scientific discourse, something implicit in all the strands of knowledge with which the natural and behavioural sciences supply us.

If it be asked how this activist view of human personality accords with concepts like peace and quietness, as these occur in Christian contexts, the answer would be that while admittedly these have their obvious and more superficial meanings in certain situations when men find themselves the victims of strife and noisy turmoil nevertheless, insofar as quietness and peace have permanent significance in all circumstances for the Christian, they are to be understood in terms rather of unimpeded activity.

Against a background view of personality such as that outlined above we can see something of the direction along which progress might be made with some of the problems which have arisen in our discussions. For example, suppose we ask how far and under what conditions medical treatments which imply personality changes (leucotomy, hormone treatment and so on) should be prescribed; how far and under what conditions medical treatment should be offered as a condition of release from prison. Plainly there will always be a consideration of social good, but the determinative question to be asked about a person will always be whether the treatment in question is likely to give him greater opportunity (albeit over a more restricted, or in some cases a markedly different, range of behaviour possibilities) for self-realization, in other words, for self-disclosure, for those moments of vision in which each of us finds freedom, spontaneity and fulfilment.

Closely related are such questions as the conditions under which universal medication should be prescribed (for example fluoride in water), or other measures introduced by the State, extending at one end of the spectrum to biological and chemical warfare and, ultimately, to control of personality by the State. Again, the crucial question—albeit in a social context—is whether and how far there will be increased

131

opportunities for that kind of self-realization which is afforded by the inspiration of a moral ideal or the pioneering of a vision.

Another group of problems arises around the morality of medical experimentation. Have we the right, and if so under what conditions, to conduct medical experiments on human beings? This area includes self-experimentation as well as the compulsory testing of human biological materials such as blood or urine for drugs. The question of parallels between the use of drugs, alcohol and cigarettes might well be opened up by asking in every case how far the chemical factors involved assist self-realization in the way we have interpreted it and when it is set against a wide-ranging social background. For the Christian, self-realization will be explicated and spelt out in terms of an exploration of the concepts and patterns current in the tradition of the Church, seen as that which all Christian doctrine has endeavoured to preserve and express, though since it is a living tradition it is something which must be constantly open to further exploration and development.

The significance of education, when seen as another means of changing human personality, can be understood along the lines we have already drawn. For education at its best is a process of self-realization, a development of personal maturity around such skills, aptitudes and abilities as any one of us possesses. Looked at in this way, the point of all instruction and training must be to make principles or knowledge one's own, to incorporate them into oneself in and through moments of self-disclosure, moments of intuition when there is genuine encountering between teacher and taught, and genuine learning, where 'genuine' is understood in terms of self-involvement rather than conditioned reflex action or indoctrination. The inculcation of habits, in the same way as the use of leucotomy or hormone treatment, can only be for the provision of some kind of stable background from which spontaneity and self-realization may better emerge. To say, for example in moral education, that people best pick up compassion by contagion is only to say that in order to inculcate a genuine sense of compassion instances of compassionate behaviour must be so presented as to lead to a disclosure, that which provides for a genuine encountering of precisely such an elusive, spontaneous, yet self-involving, inward kind as makes the metaphor of contagion appropriate.

This then in outline is a Christian view of personality which is offered as possibly providing a fruitful background against which there could be further discussion of medical-social problems and possibilities, as well as being a view of personality that could be a presupposition of all genuine education.

15: Particular Topics: General Discussion

IMPRISONMENT

This chapter of the book concerns the working party's discussions of three processes—Imprisonment, Religious Conversion and Education—through which changes in personality may occur.

Can medical interference, or punishment according to the law, or religious conversion, change personality? As far as the law and medical interference are concerned, a case is on record of a person described as a sexual psychopath who, whilst before the courts on a charge of sexual assault, applied to the judge for permission to have 'an operation to change him from a male into a female'. The judge, Lord Chief Justice Goddard declined to comment. In effect this means that the courts have no authority to permit or advise such an operation, the problem must be dealt with by the administrative machinery—the Prison Department of the Home Office.

Would a man's freedom be more invaded by a long prison sentence or by the lifelong irreversible effects of absence of male sex hormone following castration? Lawyers generally feel that though on release from prison a man might be different, he would still be master of the citadel of his own soul, whereas hormone treatment might cause far-reaching and irreversible changes in his personality, attacking his internal freedom; and this they (the lawyers) rightly oppose. Their point is that prison interferes only with social freedom. Re-education in prison is one thing because the man can take it or leave it; medical interference is another because it may take away this choice. On the other hand, and in the interest of sheer practicality and not considering retribution, there might be more chance of protecting society more effectively, and reforming the individual concerned, by using hormone treatment than by imprisonment. Only if punishment is seen as retribution would this suggestion fall down; if prisons were really intended to help towards the better life the suggestion would be practicable.

Psychiatrists, on the other hand, may see the legal distinction as too sharp and hold that detention in prison is likely to affect the prisoner's personality at least as much as hormonal changes. Naturally much depends on the conditions in any particular prison, but as the extreme of solitary confinement is accepted as very damaging to personality one may conclude that even milder restrictions have some effect. And even the more enlightened prisons can scarcely be regarded yet as ideal places for developing a prisoner's capacity for making free choices.

RELIGIOUS CONVERSION

Some part of religious conversion could certainly not be described as a free acceptance of a change of personality. The account of St Paul's conversion tells of an overwhelming force *ab extra*. To speak of acceptance or choice in Paul's case is to stretch language. The Augustinian theology of irresistible grace is more apposite. An essentially liberal concept of personality would resent the idea of an overwhelming force as an invasion whereas, from the religious point of view, conversion is the one situation in which such invasion is essential. From this point of view it would be argued that the force of irresistible grace, far from being oppressive, is the force of love. Internal unconscious changes are also necessary for a conversion to have lasting effects; this is confirmed by another aspect of Paul's conversion: the gradual way in which changes occurred. A lengthy process took place between the time of the incident on the Damascus road and Paul's eventual changed behaviour. Beliefs about an overwhelming force and some of St Augustine's theorizing about irresistible grace can both be regarded as ways of paying backhanded compliments to God. The basic intention of such doctrines is to give the initiative to God.

EDUCATION*

Personality can be strengthened as well as damaged. If the concept of personality as an owned or integrating activity is used, then strengthening implies redirection through, for example, education.†

The possible effects of modern scientific methods of education may teach us something about the nature of personality. Psychiatrists have been known to apologize for having effected a change without meaning to, and the same might apply to teachers.

Is education in a different category from medical treatments in effecting changes in personality? One difference is that the subject of education—the child—is immature and cannot achieve maturity unless subjected to influences which in the nature of the case he cannot resist. A distinction must therefore be made between adult and child, and this view was reproduced in a government report.[1]

There are many different sorts of educational processes and methods. These can, broadly, be divided into methods with and methods without subjective involvement. The former include instruction, example, conditioning, drill, and learning by rote, whereas the latter aim at developing the child's powers of reasoning, judgment and learning. In moral education subjective involvement is vital, the most important

* We are grateful to Professor R. S. Peters for his contributions to this section.
† See also pp. 129 and 132.

work being done by the subject himself. He has something put before him *to be done*, which is discrepant with what he has done before, and he discovers by degrees that he can do this next thing. Conditioning and so on are only extrinsic aids, inadequate to account for the transmission of beliefs.

One of the aims of education is sometimes said to be to give a child freedom to develop, to equip him so that he can assess and then accept or reject beliefs or dogmas, to equip him to make choices. A child cannot think ethically unless he is offered some principles or notions of justice and fairness. He probably needs to be given experience of these in specific ways. But it is unrealistic and may be dangerous to offer a child freedom of choice without the equipment with which to choose. In such circumstances, one might become committed to some kind of aim based on the view that one brand of moral education is better than another when it gives a capacity for judgment and appraisal which the other denies. It was repeatedly emphasized that education is concerned with the development of the ability to reason for oneself.

Some members of the working party thought that moral education cannot occur unless a child had been inculcated with at least some ideas and beliefs through example, habituation or instruction, from parents or teacher. In other words, teaching cannot completely exclude the assimilation of content. Other members maintained that the *good teacher* concentrates little on content and mainly on the development of ways of thinking. He considers his own ideas less important than forms of thought. His concern is that his pupils learn forms of reasoning and thinking—scientific for scientific matters, moral for moral matters and so on. But an educator would not remain neutral in the face of falsity or unsound argument, against which he would be passionately committed. The educator is influencing the child by more than logic; he is using his attitude to and relationship with the child, even if he is unaware of what he is doing.

The members of the group were divided in the emphasis they placed on forms of reasoning and assimilation of content respectively. To develop a 'good life' people had to be encouraged at least to act as though they accepted as true that which there was good reason to accept as true. Some moral rules were essential. An individual who would not act except on what he had worked out for himself would be a moral imbecile and a menace to society. There must be a willingness to accept authority on some occasions. It was agreed that in the early stages of a child's education some learning of content through habituation is probably necessary but that to prolong this would be disastrous, especially on moral issues. Aristotle had written that early habituation was needed to develop certain tendencies in preparation for the awakening of understanding. If one waits until a child can understand courage

135

before he can act courageously (or compassion before he can be compassionate) he may never be able to commit himself. But if he is indoctrinated to be brave in all situations, he will not later be equipped to make up his mind about whether to act courageously in a situation where such an action would be not brave but foolhardy. The Spartans were not courageous as we understand the word, but trained to their performance. At the other pole, the Athenians (according to Plato) were brought up to exercise reason so autonomously that they failed in any situation demanding commitment of character. A proper education would balance the two extremes and develop a child's reason in order for him to appreciate principles and his strength of character for him to act on them.

The *good doctor* shares some of the features of the good teacher. He does not describe his own inner convictions (value judgments) to the patient, though he may suggest the difficult concept that absolute conditions for a satisfactory life do exist. But, like the good teacher, he is absolutely intolerant of 'bad' medical practice. There are occasions, for doctor and teacher, when it is right not to conceal one's own convictions, but even then children (or patients) do not have to accept them; there should never be coercion.

What is the position of the *good priest* concerning forms of thought and the assimilation of content? Theologians in the past have shown no reserve about their personal convictions in the sense of (*a*) not concealing their commitment to principle, and (*b*) not stopping with content as such but trying to give it a sense of permanent fixity thus creating a prescriptive theology. Some such individuals still exist today. But increasingly in recent years, and in the context of searching for what is distinctive about theology (now that logical differences between theology and science have been more clearly defined), theologians are tending to emphasize the factor of self-involvement as an important element in moral and religious education. What a person 'sees' when the penny drops and a moral challenge is discerned may be of deep, even transcendent, concern. Theologians are now trying to express in terms of behaviour patterns the self-involvement which occurs in response to a transcendental disclosure; they are not content simply to point it out. Further, incarnational Christianity tries to integrate all this, in contrast to the so-called spiritual religions which disparage content and the secular creeds which are concerned with content alone. The good theologian supports that spontaneous response to inspiration in which freedom, self-fulfilment and maturity are found. Thus, just as educators and doctors recognize their responsibility for intervening occasionally, even at a non-rational level, at certain stages of an individual's growth or health, the Church similarly accepts that there are times when it must be authoritative.

Possible common factors between moral and scientific experience were discussed. In what ways can religious education and understanding be compared with scientific education and understanding (which depend on the child's wish to grasp and express)? A religious person would claim that in religious education the child is responding to something which inspires, rather than absorbing uncritically 'what the teacher says'. Theology has a concept of education which matches its concept of personality. Can content in religious teaching be assessed in the same way as scientific content? Would it help, for example, to examine for truth or falsehood the sayings (hymns, prayers, dogma, liturgy) and actions of religious figures? Unfortunately there are no quantitative tests or standard models of experience for assessing the truth of religious claims. This is not to say that there are no criteria for assessing theological discourse (*v. i.*).

A religious educator may have to present a tradition to which he subscribes so that his pupils can choose whether to use it as a starting point. But he will do this more by example than by words. Tradition carries elements that cannot be appreciated by everyone in a particular generation but which individuals at any time can apprehend, make their own and respond to. The theologian can never work in isolation. In theology (and in art and science) progress was made by men first disciplined in a tradition. Unfortunately this can lead to tradition being handed down in an oppressive way (this has endlessly compromised religion in the past) and is very different from handing on a tradition in a more open way. Tradition is thus an ambiguous term. For some it is fixed and final: a deposit of faith whose developments are already contained implicitly so that development consists only of consistent deductions. For others the tradition, the *depositum fidei*, is more elusive. Similarly, in science, certain questions can be neither asked nor examined without tradition. But again there is no objective way of deciding whether a tradition (or dogma or belief) should be accepted or rejected. If some theologians hold on too stubbornly to traditions, some scientists throw them over too quickly.

Until recently theology saw itself as monolithic, with a sense of being single-stranded and the absolute truth. In the past twenty years it has been considered as a more variegated structure. This multiple character, made more evident by recent controversy, has brought with it the need for a more coherent picture and better bridging concepts. Although this changing view is necessarily accompanied by a certain lack of clarity there are some criteria for judging theological discourse. These are formal criteria (of coherence, consistency, comprehensiveness and simplicity) and material criteria (links with the world, empiric fit). In these circumstances, where theology has its own distinctive forms of reasoning, it can be incorporated in a coherent picture of education which embraces science and morality as well as itself. This is not surprising when—and indeed because—these different types of education share the same concept of personality.

REFERENCE

1. Cmnd 3342 (1967). *Report of the Lord Chancellor's Committee on the Age of Majority* (Chairman: Sir John Latey). London: HMSO.

16: Recurrent Themes: General Discussion

DURING our discussions we found the same medico-moral topics being raised on different occasions and in different contexts. In this section we gather together some of these recurrent topics, of interest and importance in their own right, and examine some of the issues and considerations which their discussion raised.

THE INDIVIDUAL AND SOCIETY

How can we rate the relative values of an individual personality on the one hand and the safety of society on the other? To what extent should the rights of a man who may be a danger to the community in which he lives be protected? To what extent should the right to non-conformity be defended and by what criteria should it be assessed? Normally the principle of *necessity* (the need of my neighbour) governs these problems, but there are conflicting necessities according to whether we consider the individual, ourselves, an other or society. To punish a man might protect society but harm the man himself. How far should social needs influence the medical treatment of a patient? To what extent, for example, should the secondary changes in personality that follow certain medical or surgical treatments be set against saving life or improving health (examples are aversion treatment for homosexuality and castration for certain sexual deviations)? If the probabilities of undesirable changes in personality after a given procedure (such as castration) and of the dangers to society without this procedure are known, at what point is it permissible to infringe (medically, socially or legally) personal liberty for the sake of public good?

To answer these questions we first looked for a definition of liberty in this context. In our non-ideal world it is debatable if free consent (by the patient) for such procedures as castration, sterilization, leucotomy, or new, untried medical treatments is a reliable safeguard. The concept of free consent is itself closely linked to the concept of personality, which cannot be described solely in terms of its psychophysical properties. This concept (of personality) needs to be greatly enlarged to include such notions as freedom (or liberty), responsibility, *mens rea*, social interdependence and natural rights. Other areas in which the rights of an individual might conflict with those of society concern such protests as taking drugs, conscientious objection to war, and madness. The failure of contemporary society to meet the needs of those whose

139

nonconformism takes these forms must have been one of the original causes of the protests.

THE DOCTOR-PATIENT RELATIONSHIP

The doctor's responsibility for his patient

An applied science such as Medicine cannot be completely objective. Personal involvement is inevitable (at the simplest level this is just the doctor's wish to help and the patient's wish to be helped). The doctor's responsibility is to the whole patient and to his environment—family, occupation and social setting—in so far as it affects him. Doctors are currently trying to return to this Hippocratic view from the limitations of the mechanistic attitudes of fifty years ago, and see their responsibilities as to the patient, his family and society, in that order. If the prime responsibility of the doctor to do what is 'best' for his patient is ignored then, in our non-ideal society, the ultimate result could be totalitarian control. But this order of priorities raises many problems. What is best for the patient, and for his mental and emotional as well as his physical health? Who decides this? We cannot even, at this stage, define mental and emotional health. A hopelessly handicapped patient may be resuscitated only to live a life of misery and/or be rejected by his family; or such a patient may survive to break up a stable home. But who should decide when a handicap is hopeless? This problem arises in connexion with the treatment and management of children with previously untreatable congenital defects (spina bifida, mongolism), of senile patients, and of patients resuscitated after acute medical (cardiac infarction, renal failure and so on) or surgical (for example, car accidents) trauma. The patient's own views about life and death as well as those of his family and of society are all relevant to this problem. If a conflict (humanitarian or economic) exists between the value of two individuals, only one of whom can survive, then who should define value and on what grounds? The doctor's strength has always been his devotion to his patient to the exclusion of others and of himself. The training of medical students emphasizes this. Only in one situation is it widely although not unanimously agreed that one class of patient should be preferred—the sick mother is kept alive at the expense of her unborn foetus. Only in exceptional circumstances, such as war or epidemics, has the doctor, in the past, had to choose to treat one patient and not another. But recent advances in medical research (for example, transplant surgery) and problems of overpopulation will now make this choice increasingly common.

The doctor's changing role

Traditionally, doctors have been concerned with restoring their patients' physical health and not with what the patients would make of this once it was restored (a broken arm must be treated even if it is subsequently used to kill). This led to the tradition (formalized by Henri Dunant when he founded the Red Cross in 1859 but probably in existence in practice before then) that an army's medical services would treat all sick and wounded, including the enemy. Such traditional behaviour is supported by mutual interest. Disregard of it by the Japanese in World War II was a shock to Western opinion for it underlined the different standards that exist in the East and the West.

Recently, more inclusive concepts of mental health and disease have made us question whether the traditional aim still holds. For if the doctor's aim is still that the patient should be restored to full health, which would now mean mental as well as physical health, then the doctor must be sure what mental health is. And there is as yet no satisfactory definition of mental health. Further, the doctor is likely to try to restore the patient to the sort of mental health of which he (the doctor) approves. Thus he may influence the patient's subsequent behaviour. In this way a difference from the traditional ideas has arisen.

But a new situation may occur in the treatment of mental illness in practice although the doctor has applied the old standards in theory. It is sometimes suggested that the psychiatrist's job is to free the patient from his inhibitions, thus allowing full emotional development. This raises the problems just formulated about the definition of mental health and of the psychiatrist's value judgments. Another difficulty is that improvement in some things may sometimes only be achieved by sacrificing abilities in others. Castration is a case in point. Fair legal treatment for a mentally sick offender may also repress his personality. A forger or exhibitionist may be cured of his deviancy in so far as his maladaptive behaviour disappears, but be permanently depressed in consequence. A person who wants to change his sex may be dissuaded, or a prostitute reformed, with resultant intractable depression.

OTHER PROFESSIONAL-PERSONAL RELATIONSHIPS

Lawyer-client

Lawyers generally accept that every right (for example, the client's right to consult) connotes a duty (that is, his duty to pay). Solicitors and barristers tend to act pragmatically although in theory they would consider that thereby they forward an ideal of justice. How far do they believe that self-interest is a universal (and the only) motive? In jurisprudence, at least in theory, the law, community responsibility and natural law may coincide: in practice they do not. In the administration of the law, one bad decision can be overlooked or re-interpreted and, in a subsequent series of cases, new principles can be gradually evolved by the courts. Thus some aspects of the law today, for example the handling of delinquent children, would have been unrealizable 150 years ago.

Priest-parishioner

The priest's functions have changed radically with changes in ecclesiastical and social contexts. Today his function in hearing confession is conceived as being to do with the penitent's total well-being (what is best for the penitent). He may be expected, or expect himself, to be a social worker or educationalist and needs special training for these new roles. The priest's qualified privilege at law (of not divulging what is told him in confession) rests on the supposition that no sin undivulged must be allowed to jeopardize the man's eternal salvation. In the Middle Ages, when the Church acted also as the agent of society for the enforcement of morals (*custos morum*), a priest would regularly refuse absolution until the penitent had submitted to penance, that is, to open correction, expensive or painful or both. Today, if the priest learns of undivulged crime, he can do no more than put moral suasion on the penitent to declare himself to the police. Similarly, there is now only an attenuated and residual sense in which the priest acts on behalf of the body corporate (the Church): that in healing one member he is helping the whole body to health; or, *per contra*, that the health of the whole body requires that the putrid member be cut off, that is, excommunicated. This change in role has created as many problems for the priest as a similar change has for the doctor.

PHILOSOPHICAL COMMENTS

Definitions of mental, emotional and spiritual health might have to include definitions of self-expression, self-fulfilment and of the purpose of life. Mental health has been defined as the ability to adapt to stress, or as maturity, but such definitions are incomplete. The quality of life is as important as its length, and a doctor may occasionally serve his patient's interests best by allowing him to die early rather than late. We have tried to identify any relevant progressive or retrogressive steps in this area.

When is it legitimate for a doctor to influence his patient's moral values? In the past such attempts have been contrary to the medical ethic, which holds that doctors should not offer advice on non-medical matters unless asked by the patient or, if the patient is incapable of asking, by his family. In this respect doctors are clearly different from, say, missionaries or politicians. Some doctors have left this traditional position and now advise on matters of public health (for example, smoking, venereal infection, alcoholism and drug addiction). Confusion may arise, for the community and for the doctors themselves, if this new role of public health adviser is not clearly distinguished from the traditional role of personal physician to one particular patient.

NEW PRINCIPLES FOR DEFINING THE DOCTOR'S RESPONSIBILITIES

After lengthy discussion it was suggested that some attempts could be made to formulate principles dispassionately and theoretically, and at a time and place distant from the occasion when an urgent decision on a particular patient must be made. As well as the doctor's duty to his patient, duties arising from his medical skills, and from the state of medical and scientific expertise at any given time, are all relevant but these issues are no longer solely medical. The decisions cannot now be left entirely to the medical profession, who themselves may need help from other professions. Similarly, the community itself may seek help from the doctor. Changing circumstances may require that there are two types of doctor, a personal doctor for the patient and another doctor whose prime duty is to the community. The patient and his personal doctor may sometimes have to accept that the community's needs come first. The two possible different types of doctor and the sorts of training they need should be further differentiated and such training implemented. If there is conflict of interests, as may increasingly occur, there should be some neutral body to adjudicate. Theoretical principles might be formulated by this neutral body which would consist of medical and non-medical members. The latter personnel might appropriately include sociologists, economists, lawyers, philosophers, theologians, social workers, probation officers and magistrates. The existence of such a mixed advisory group would safeguard the doctor's role as the advocate of his patient's interests and of no other person's.

We agreed that the doctor, in principle, must not try, or be expected to try, to represent both sides (his patient and the community). When interests conflict he must take and show that he takes his patient's side. All the members of the group, medical and non-medical, were in strong agreement that if the patient's personal doctor ceased to support him— or if this appeared to be so—the whole ethics of the profession, intact since Hippocrates, would be radically (and adversely) changed.

17: Epilogue

I. T. RAMSEY

In days past, medical and scientific discoveries used to start peripherally in the community and then move centrally to scientific laboratories for investigation before being put to use in a professional way. For example, from the foxglove, originally an old wives' cure for dropsy, came digitalis and digoxin. One of the distinctive features of contemporary society is that the movement is now in the opposite direction: from small scientific areas of research into the community at large. The adoption of scientific advances for use in society, once secured by a process of refining, now occurs by a process of spreading out. This means that the initiative for the application of scientific advances now often rests with non-medical technologists. This raises potential dangers, not least in the field of scientific medicine. These dangers arise partly because the non-medical technologist will not necessarily have been brought up with that professional ethic which has for so long been inculcated, implicitly if not explicitly, in medical training and tradition. There is the further danger that the non-medical technologist is likely to be politically more powerful than a member of the medical profession. The point need not be laboured for it is an obvious feature of the society in which we live. There are countless ways in which medical research can be or is being used with the express purpose of inflicting harm and/or making money. Examples are the use of psychological techniques for brainwashing, of CS gas in matters of public order and the spreading use of drugs. And medical research, like technological progress, can sometimes, even accidentally, work to the obvious disadvantage of society, as occurs with pollution from oil tankers or fall-out from the testing of nuclear weapons.

All this makes it the more important that there should be in society an alertness to moral issues raised by developments in science, and a deeper and broader sense of social responsibility. Broader, since the field is being constantly broadened by scientific discovery and research; deeper, because it will need novel moral insights to match the novelty of the problems with which developments in science, and in particular scientific medicine, present us. Crucial to all discussions in this field will be the scientist's view of personality, which will largely determine, consciously or not, his attitudes to problems and the decisions he makes.

Looking back on our discussions in the past three years or so, it might be said that we have tried to formulate some of the moral issues

145

raised, in one or two important areas, by contemporary developments in scientific medicine. We have at no stage tried to give anything like a scientific account of personality. Indeed, some of the necessary disciplines (for example, psychology) for such an account were not represented in our group. But we have tried to show in terms of a number of fields how scientific disciplines are relevant to such questions, as: 'What are man's possibilities?' and 'In what ways can human personality be changed?' But such questions lead immediately to further questions: 'Who decides to change a man's personality?' 'On what grounds can we legitimately bring about personality changes?' and 'How would we appraise the changes in human personality that might be brought about by science, education or religion?'.

It is by moving outward in this way that we hope our discussions have shown that scientific developments must necessarily be set in a framework of broader ideas. Besides being someone about whom scientific disciplines can tell us a great deal, each man has also a distinctive personality, an autonomy, an interest which must be recognized, and possibilities which have to be respected, and his relationships with other persons, whether professional or as a fellow member of society, have to be worked out with patience and thoroughness. Man is a moral agent as well as the topic of scientific inquiry; a subject exercising moral decision as well as an object of investigation giving rise to scientific conclusions.

If we were to gather together some of the phrases which in our discussions have come to characterize the non-scientific aspect of personality, phrases which in this way have pointed to the non-scientific ingredients of personality, they would, we believe, point to a dynamic view of personality, to personality as an owned or integrating activity, an activity which is outgoing and effective, an activity in exercising which we come to ourselves. Within such a view of personality the multiple understandings of science readily fit. Man is an embodied activity who seeks self-expression, self-realization and self-fulfilment, and never discovers these better than when making genuinely moral decisions. Whatever medical science can or cannot do, it respects a person's desire for self-expression and self-fulfilment. Further, it must recognize that it is in coming to moral decisions that men most characteristically can hope to find themselves, gain access to themselves, and discover in the case of each man a unique subjectivity talked of in terms such as freedom, spontaneity and independence. So science must work in a framework of morality if it seeks to give an adequate account of human personality. At the same time it must be realized that such freedom and fulfilment and self-expression and uniqueness are only realized in interdependence as part of a community.

In short, as we see it, a scientific view of personality must always leave room for personality as creative activity. It must never deny, or be used to suppress, that creative activity which is not only basic to our concept of personality but essential to the very development of science itself, let alone to advances in the humanities. This is the view of personality which is a *sine qua non* for the well-being of a society in which all of us need to fulfil ourselves in interdependence.

ACKNOWLEDGEMENTS

The editors wish to record their gratitude to the two people who have carried the considerable secretarial burden in connexion with this volume, Mrs M. M. Harrison and Mrs F. R. Spencer-Lush.

Contributors

Permanent members of the working party and authors of the presentations in the book.

I. T. RAMSEY

Rt Revd Lord Bishop of Durham, since 1966; Hon. Fellow of Christ's College, Cambridge and of Oriel College, Oxford, since 1967.

Late Scholar of Christ's College, Cambridge. 1st class: mathematical tripos pt i, 1936, moral sciences tripos pt iia, 1938, and theological tripos pt ii, 1939. Formerly Chaplain of Christ's College, Cambridge, 1943–49; Fellow 1944–51; Tutor 1949–51; Nolloth Professor of the Philosophy of the Christian Religion and Fellow of Oriel College, Oxford, 1951–66. *Special interests:* relationships between theology, philosophy and science; moral education; communication between theologists and non-theologists.

Publications include: *Religious Language* (1957). London: Student Christian Movement Press. *Biology and Personality* (1965). (ed.) Oxford: Blackwell.

S. CROWN

Consultant Psychiatrist, The London Hospital and Medical College, since 1966.

Trained first as an academic psychologist (Ph.D. London University, 1949), followed by training in medicine (Middlesex Hospital, 1959), psychiatry and psychoanalysis. Member, Royal Colleges of Physicians and of Psychiatrists. *Special concerns:* breaking down barriers between disciplines. *Special interests:* psychotherapy and counselling methods; medical education; medico-legal problems; the assessment of personality.

Publications include: *Essential Principles of Psychiatry* (1971). London: Pitman. (Textbook for students.)

G. R. DUNSTAN

F. D. Maurice Professor of Moral and Social Theology, King's College London since 1967.

Graduated in History (1st class) Leeds University, 1938. Canon Theologian, Leicester Cathedral, since 1966; Priest in Ordinary to the Queen, since 1964. Previous positions include Minor Canon, St George's Chapel, Windsor Castle, 1955–59, Westminster Abbey, 1959–67; Sec., Church of England Council for Social Work, 1955–63, Church Assembly Joint Board of Studies, 1963–66; Select Preacher, University of Cambridge, 1960. *Special interests:* social and ethical problems; the family; theological history.

Publications include: *The Register of Edmund Lacy, Bishop of Exeter, 1420–1455* (5 vols, ed.) (1963–1972). London: Canterbury and York Society. Ed. *Crucible,* 1962–66, *Theology,* since 1965.

M. A. FALCONER

Director of the Neurosurgical Unit of Guy's and Maudsley (now and King's) Hospitals, London, since 1950; and Hon. Consultant Neurosurgeon, King's College Hospital.

Graduated in Medicine, Otago University, Dunedin, New Zealand, 1934; Fellow, Royal College of Surgeons (England), 1935. Formerly held positions in departments of Surgery and Neurosurgery at Universities of Otago and Oxford, and at Mayo Foundation and Johns Hopkins Hospital, US. *Special interests:* surgical treatment of epilepsy.

Publications include: *Surgical Treatment of Drug-Resistant Epilepsy due to Mesial Temporal Sclerosis* (1968). *Archiv. Neurol. Complications Related to Delayed Haemorrhage after Hemispherectomy* (1969). *J. Neurosurg.* (both jointly).

L. P. R. FOURMAN (died 1968)

Professor of Clinical Investigation, University of Leeds and Physician to Leeds General Infirmary, 1963–68.

Graduate of London University and Guy's Hospital, London, 1941; Fellow, Royal College of Physicians; British Army in India, 1945–46. Held positions in academic medicine at Guy's Hospital and the Universities of Oxford, Cambridge and Wales; Rockefeller Travelling Fellow, 1948–49; polylinguist. *Special interests:* calcium metabolism and malabsorption states; medical education; international cooperation in medical research.

Publications include: *Calcium Metabolism and the Bone* (1960). Oxford: Blackwell.

T. FREEMAN

Consultant Psychiatrist, Holywell Hospital, Antrim and City Hospital, Belfast, N. Ireland, since 1968 and Consultant, Hampstead Child Therapy Clinic, London, England.

Graduated in Medicine, Queen's University, Belfast, 1942; Fellow, Royal College of Physicians (Edinburgh), 1969; Member, British Psycho-Analytical Society. Formerly Consultant Psychiatrist at hospitals in Belfast, Dundee and Glasgow. *Special interests:* use of psychoanalytic concepts in the management of schizophrenia and other psychoses; integration of psychoanalytic principles with the teaching and practice of psychiatry.

Publications include: *Psychopathology of the Psychoses* (1969). London: Tavistock. Chapter on learning component in dynamic psychotherapy in *Ciba Fdn Symp. The Role of Learning in Psychotherapy* (1968). London: Churchill.

RAYMOND GREENE

Hon. Consultant Physician, Royal Northern and New End Hospitals, since 1966; Chairman, Heinemann Medical Books Ltd.

Graduated from Oxford University and Westminster Hospital, London, 1929; Fellow, Royal College of Physicians and Chevalier, Légion d'Honneur; member of Everest Expedition, 1933. Formerly in charge of Endocrine Clinic at Westminster Hospital and Physician and Endocrinologist, Royal Northern and New End Hospitals. *Special interests:* effects of high altitude and exposure to cold, particularly on endocrine function; medical book publishing.

Publications include: *Myasthenia Gravis* (1969). Philadelphia: Lipincott. *Human Hormones* (1970). London: Weidenfeld and Nicolson.

R. M. HARE

White's Professor of Moral Philosophy and Fellow of Corpus Christi College, Oxford, since 1966.

Graduated in Lit. Hum. (1st class), Oxford University, 1942. Served in Royal Artillery and Indian Mountain Artillery in World War II; prisoner of war in Far East, 1942–45. Formerly Fellow and Tutor in Philosophy, Balliol College, Oxford, 1947–66; Visiting Fellow or Professor at Universities of Princeton and Michigan, and Australian National University, Canberra; member of National Road Safety Advisory Council, 1966–68. *Special interests:* the application of philosophy to practical moral problems; town planning and transport problems.

Publications include: *The Language of Morals* (1952). London: Oxford University Press. *Freedom and Reason* (1963). London: Oxford University Press.

SIR DENIS HILL

Professor of Psychiatry, Institute of Psychiatry, London University and Hon. Consultant at Bethlem Royal and Maudsley Hospitals, since 1966.

Graduate of London University and St Thomas's Hospital, London. Fellow, Royal Colleges of Physicians and of Psychiatrists. Formerly Physician in Psychological Medicine, King's College Hospital and Senior Lecturer, Department of Clinical Neurophysiology, Institute of Psychiatry, 1947–61; Professor of Psychiatry, Middlesex Hospital Medical School, 1961–66; Member, Med. Res. Council, 1956–60, Central Health Service Council, 1961–67; Chairman, Mental Health Advisory Committee, 1960–66; Crown Rep. Gen. Med. Council, 1961; Rock Carling Fellow, 1969; Ernest Jones Lecturer (British Psycho-Analytical Soc.), 1970. *Special interests:* training and educational objectives in psychiatry.

Publications include: *Psychiatry in Medicine in Retrospect and Prospect* (1971). London: Nuffield Provincial Hospitals Trust.

T. E. JAMES

Professor, Faculty of Laws, King's College London, Dean and Head of Department, since 1970; Barrister at Law, Member of Gray's Inn.

Graduated in Law, London University, 1933, followed by Ph.D. (London) and B.C.L. (Bachelor of Criminal Law) from Oxford University. *Special interests:* the law relating to children; penology and property law.

Publications include: *Prostitution and the Law* (1951). London: Heinemann Medical. *Child Law* (1962). London: Sweet and Maxwell. Reiwald, P. *Society and Its Criminals* [trans. from German by James, T. E. (1949. London: Heinemann Medical; 1950, New York: Int. Universities Press)]. Chapters on English law relating to psychiatry in various books, e.g. in *The Pathology and Treatment of Sexual Deviation* (1964). London: Oxford University Press.

C. R. B. JOYCE

Member of Medical Department, CIBA-GEIGY Ltd, Basel, since 1969.

Graduated in Moral Sci., University of Cambridge, 1949. Formerly Lecturer and Reader in Psycho-Pharmacology, University of London (London Hospital Medical College); member of Hallucinogen Subcommittee (Chairman, Lady Wootton) of Advisory Committee on Drug Dependence, 1966–68. *Special interests:* multidisciplinary studies in pharmacology, psychiatry and medicine; assessment of psychotropic drugs.

Publications include: *Psychopharmacology: Dimensions and Perspectives* (ed.) (1968). London: Tavistock. *Treatment or Diagnosis: a Study of Repeat Prescriptions in General Practice* (1970). London: Tavistock (jointly).

S. LEVINE

Associate Professor of Psychiatry, Stanford University Medical Center, California, since 1962.

Graduated in Psychology, New York University. Formerly held positions in Departments of Psychology in the US; and in Department of Neuroendocrinology, Institute of Psychiatry, London, England, 1960–61. *Special interests:* neuroendocrinology and developmental psychobiology and physiology; effects of infantile experiences in animals on later sexual development and behaviour.

Publications include: Paper on hormones and conditioning in *Nebraska Symposium on Motivation* (1968). Lincoln: University of Nebraska Press. Paper on *Sexual Differentiation of the Brain and Its Experimental Control* (1962). *J. Physiol., Lond.* (jointly with G. W. Harris).

B. G. MITCHELL

Nolloth Professor of the Philosophy of the Christian Religion, Oxford University and Fellow of Oriel College, Oxford, since 1968.

Graduated in Lit. Hum., Oxford University, 1939; Royal Navy, 1940–46. Formerly Lecturer, Christ Church, Oxford and Fellow and Tutor in Philosophy, Keble College, Oxford. Visiting Professor and/or Lecturer, Princeton, and Cambridge and Birmingham (England), Universities. *Special interests:* relationships between philosophy, theology and science.

Publications include: *Law, Morality and Religion in a Secular Society* (1967). London: Oxford University Press. *Neutrality and Commitment* (1968). Oxford: Clarendon Press. *Logic* (1957). (ed.) London: Allen and Unwin.

RUTH PORTER

Deputy Director, Ciba Foundation, London; psychotherapist.

Graduate of Edinburgh University (Medicine), 1948; Member, Royal College of Physicians and Affiliate, Royal College of Psychiatrists. Formerly Medical Registrar Addenbrookes Hospital, Cambridge, England and University College Hospital of the West Indies, Jamaica; House Physician, Victoria Hospital for Children (St George's Hospital), London. *Special interests:* small multidisciplinary groups and conferences; relationships between medicine, psychiatry and psychoanalysis; psychoanalytic psychotherapy.

Publications: editor Ciba Foundation symposia and study groups since 1964.

G. K. STÜRUP

Superintendent, Herstedvester Detention Centre, Albertslund, Denmark, since 1942.

Graduated in Medicine, 1929. Formerly held positions in psychiatry and medicine in Denmark and Greenland. Gold Medal, Faculty of Philosophy, Copenhagen University and Fellow, Rockefeller Foundation, 1934; Visiting Lecturer, Boston University, 1953; Visiting Scholar, Center for Studies in Criminal Justice, the Law School, University of Chicago, 1966–67. *Special interests:* personality in collaborators in World War II; treatment for mentally abnormal and other prisoners; penal law reform.

Publications include: *Sex Offenses: the Scandinavian Experience in Law and Contemporary Problems* (1960). Durham, N.C.: Duke University Press. *Treating the 'Untreatable' Chronic Criminals at Herstedvester, Denmark* (1968). Baltimore: John Hopkins Press and *Treatment of Sexual Offenders at Herstedvester, Denmark* (1968). Copenhagen: Munksgaard (Isaac Ray Lectures). Ciba Foundation Annual Lecture, 1967, *Will This Man be Dangerous?* in *Ciba Fdn Symp. The Mentally Abnormal Offender* (1968). London: Churchill.

R. F. TREDGOLD

Physician in charge, Department of Psychiatry, University College Hospital, London, since 1952.

Graduate of Cambridge University; trained in Medicine and Psychiatry at Cambridge and University College Hospital, London. Fellow, Royal Colleges of Medicine and of Psychiatry; Hon. Consultant Psychiatrist to Army at Home. Formerly Psychiatrist to S.E. Met. Reg. Hosp. Board, England; Adviser in Psychiatry, Allied Land Forces, S.E. Asia; President, Int. Committee Occupational Mental Health. *Special interests:* directing a psychiatric department occupied in treating patients; teaching psychiatry to medical and other students; the uses of psychiatry in occupational medicine; encouraging collaboration between various professions concerned with mental health and illness.

Publications include: *Human Relations in Modern Industry* (2nd edn, 1963). New York: International Universities Press. *U.C.H. Notes on Psychiatry* (1971). London: Duckworth (jointly).

O. H. WOLFF

Nuffield Professor of Child Health, University of London and Consultant Physician to the Hospital for Sick Children, Great Ormond Street, since 1965.

Graduate of Cambridge University and University College Hospital, London. Fellow, Royal College of Physicians. Formerly Registrar in Medicine and Reader in Paediatrics and Child Health in the University of Birmingham, England. *Special interests:* abnormalities of lipid metabolism in children; childhood obesity; the sick or mentally retarded child and his family.

Publications include: chapter on disturbances of serum lipoproteins in *Endocrine and Genetic Diseases of Childhood* (1969). Philadelphia: Saunders.

G. E. W. WOLSTENHOLME

Director, Ciba Foundation, London, since its opening in 1949.

Graduate of Cambridge University and Middlesex Hospital, London. Fellow, Royal College of Physicians; Fellow, Institute of Biology; O.B.E. (mil.); Hon. LL.D. (Cambridge); Chevalier, Légion d'Honneur; Gold Medal, Italian Ministry of Education; Trustee, Developmental Sciences Trust; Member of Council (since 1961) and Chairman, Advisory Committee of Society Symposia and Special Meetings (since 1971), Royal Society of Medicine; Member of Council, Westfield College, London University, since 1965. Formerly Adviser in Transfusion and Resuscitation, Central Mediterranean, 1943–45; Organizer (1963) and Adviser (1963–64), Haile Selassie I Prize Trust, Addis Ababa; Hon. Secretary (1964–70) and President, Library Section (1968–70), Royal Society of Medicine.

Publications: chief editor, Ciba Foundation symposia, colloquia and study groups since 1950. *The Royal College of Physicians of London: Portraits* (1964). London: Churchill.

INDEX OF AUTHORS

INDEX OF SUBJECTS

Printed by William Clowes & Sons Limited, London, Colchester and Beccles